K.M.

WITHDRAWN

REGENTS RENAISSANCE DRAMA SERIES

General Editor: Cyrus Hoy
Advisory Editor: G. E. Bentley

ALL FOOLS

GEORGE CHAPMAN

All Fools

Edited by

FRANK MANLEY

UNIVERSITY OF NEBRASKA PRESS · LINCOLN

Regents Renaissance Drama Series

The purpose of the Regents Renaissance Drama Series is to provide soundly edited texts, in modern spelling, of the more significant plays of the Elizabethan, Jacobean, and Caroline theater. Each text in the series is based on a fresh collation of all sixteenth- and seventeenth-century editions. The textual notes, which appear above the line at the bottom of each page, record all substantive departures from the edition used as the copy-text. Variant substantive readings among sixteenth- and seventeenth-century editions are listed there as well. In cases where two or more of the old editions present widely divergent readings, a list of substantive variants in editions through the seventeenth century is given in an appendix. Editions after 1700 are referred to in the textual notes only when an emendation originating in some one of them is received into the text. Variants of accidentals (spelling, punctuation, capitalization) are not recorded in the notes. Contracted forms of characters' names are silently expanded in speech prefixes and stage directions, and, in the case of speech prefixes, are regularized. Additions to the stage directions of the copy-text are enclosed in brackets. Stage directions such as "within" or "aside" are enclosed in parentheses when they occur in the copy-text.

Spelling has been modernized along consciously conservative lines. "Murther" has become "murder," and "burthen," "burden," but within the limits of a modernized text, and with the following exceptions, the linguistic quality of the original has been carefully preserved. The variety of contracted forms ('em, 'am, 'm, 'um, 'hem) used in the drama of the period for the pronoun *them* are here regularly given as 'em, and the alternation between *a'th'* and *o'th'* (for *on* or *of the*) is regularly reproduced as *o'th'*. The copy-text distinction between preterite endings in -*d* and -*ed* is preserved except where the elision of *e* occurs in the penultimate syllable; in such cases, the final syllable is contracted. Thus, where the old editions read "threat'ned," those of the present series read "threaten'd." Where, in the old editions, a contracted preterite in -*y'd* would yield -*i'd* in modern spelling (as in "try'd," "cry'd," "deny'd"), the word is here given in its full form (e.g., "tried," "cried," "denied").

170015

Punctuation has been brought into accord with modern practices. The effort here has been to achieve a balance between the generally light pointing of the old editions, and a system of punctuation which, without overloading the text with exclamation marks, semicolons, and dashes, will make the often loosely flowing verse (and prose) of the original syntactically intelligible to the modern reader. Dashes are regularly used only to indicate interrupted speeches, or shifts of address within a single speech.

Explanatory notes, chiefly concerned with glossing obsolete words and phrases, are printed below the textual notes at the bottom of each page. References to stage directions in the notes follow the admirable system of the Revels editions, whereby stage directions are keyed, decimally, to the line of the text before or after which they occur. Thus, a note on 0.2 has reference to the second line of the stage direction at the beginning of the scene in question. A note on 115.1 has reference to the first line of the stage direction following line 115 of the text of the relevant scene.

CYRUS HOY

University of Rochester

Contents

List of Abbreviations

Collier	J. P. Collier, ed. *Dodsley's Old Plays*. London, 1825.
corr.	corrected
Dodsley	Robert Dodsley, ed. *A Selected Collection of Old Plays*. London, 1780.
OED	*Oxford English Dictionary*
Parrott	T. M. Parrott, ed. *The Comedies of George Chapman*. London, 1914.
Q	Thorpe's 1605 Quarto
S.D.	stage direction
Shepherd	R. H. Shepherd, ed. *The Comedies and Tragedies of George Chapman*. London, 1873.
S.P.	speech prefix
Tilley	M. P. Tilley. *A Dictionary of the Proverbs in England in the Sixteenth and Seventeenth Centuries*. Ann Arbor, 1950.
uncorr.	uncorrected

Introduction

When *All Fools* first appeared in print in 1605, the author was in jail, in danger of having his nose and ears slit for insulting the king. Ben Jonson, who was with him, writes in a letter to the Earl of Salisbury complaining of his "vile prison" and extolling the company of "a gentleman . . . one Mr. George Chapman, a learned and honest man."[1] By that time Chapman was well into middle age, a fairly well-known poet and playwright. Born near Hitchin in Hertfordshire in 1559 or 1560, his early life is obscure. According to Anthony à Wood, he "spent some time in Oxon. where he was observed to be most excellent in the Lat. and Greek tongues, but not in logic or philosophy, and therefore I presume that that was the reason he took no degree here."[2] Like Ben Jonson he may have soldiered for a time in the Low Countries. But whatever he did with his youth, in 1594, shortly after the death of Marlowe and the demise of the University Wits, he set up as a poet in London, publishing his obscure *Shadow of Night*. His first work in the theater was as a member of Henslowe's factory, and his first plays were comedies—*The Blind Beggar of Alexandria* (1596), *An Humorous Day's Mirth* (1597)—culminating in his comic masterpiece, *All Fools* (1599). Around 1600 he became chief playwright for the Children of the Chapel, gradually shifting from comedy to tragedy. He quit writing actively for the theater around 1612 and turned to his translations of Homer, installments of which had appeared as early as 1598. From 1616 until his death eighteen years later Chapman seems to have ceased writing, and we consequently know little about these last years of his life. He was by that time fifty-six years old. He complains of poverty in the few letters that survive and at one time borrowed money from a brother in order to marry a rich widow, a campaign that was not successful. According to Anthony à Wood, "He was a person of most reverend aspect, religious and temperate, qualities rarely meeting in a poet" (col.

---

[1] Cited in A. H. Bullen's article on Chapman in the *Dictionary of National Biography*. This is still the best brief life.

[2] Anthony à Wood, *Athenae Oxonienses* (London, 1815), II, col. 575.

596), and despite the evidence to the contrary, it is pleasant to believe that Oldys was right in his notes to Langbaine's *Lives* that Chapman was revered in his last days: "much resorted to by young persons of parts as a poetical chronicle: but was very choice who he admitted to him, and preserved in his own person the dignity of Poetry, which he compared to a flower of the sun, that disdains to open its leaves to the eye of a smoking taper."[3] He died in 1634 at the age of seventy-four, having "made his last exit in the parish of S. Giles's in the Fields near London."[4] A monument of Portland stone "built after the way of the old Romans" was erected over his grave by Inigo Jones, *ob honorem bonarum literorum, familiari suo.* Engraved on it were the words: "Poeta Homericus, Philosophus verus (etsi Christianus poeta)."[5] His plays were forgotten.

Yet his plays are his greatest monument—and none greater than *All Fools*, not even the magnificient *Bussy D'Ambois*, with its clouded splendor and tragic ambiguity. For *All Fools* is not only Chapman's most flawless, perfectly balanced play, it is also his most human and large-minded. His comedies and tragedies that followed are satiric and fragmented, tainted with the bitterness and revulsion we associate with the Jacobean age. *All Fools*, on the other hand, breathes the spirit of fresher and more wholesome times—the Classical, in its imitation of Terence, and the late Elizabethan, with its hearty self-confidence. Although the basic form of the play is satiric, the satire is contained and relieved by a whole-hearted gusto and respect for humanity that makes even fools like Gostanzo and Cornelio more interesting and more human for the very reason that they are such fools. And they wisely never lose their foolishness. No matter what they discover about themselves, they end as they began. Cornelio, the jealous man who has been blinded and tormented by his passion through most of the play, still thinks at the end that jealousy is "clear-eyed." And Gostanzo is still able to give him advice—wonderfully dumb, foolish advice—still believing himself to be a crafty, politic man.

The essential form of *All Fools* has to do with self-deception. It is not easily stated in a formula since the play itself is the only way to articulate it fully. But translating it into other terms, it treats of deceivers who are themselves deceived through their self-deception.

---

[3] Cited in Bullen.
[4] A. à Wood, col. 578.
[5] A. à Wood, col. 578–579.

The plot,[6] for example, turns primarily on Gostanzo's image of himself as a crafty, Machiavellian man, provident, experienced in the ways of the world, superior to all his neighbors, and the good father of an obedient son. Yet we know him as an "old, politic, dissembling knight" (I.i. 401), a garrulous fool whose tricks all backfire on him, whose obedient son is secretly a profligate, and whose sense of value is based on money alone:

> Love nothing heartily in this world but riches,
> Cast off all friends, all studies, all delights,
> All honesty, and religion for riches.
>
> (I.i. 202–204)

He advises his son that "Promises are no fetters," that "friendship's but a term" (II.i. 69, 79), and reveals his basic hypocrisy by offering his daughter-in-law (whom, admittedly, he takes for someone else's) "A twelvemonths' board for one night's lodging with her" (IV.i.99). Even at the end of the play he forgives his son only because he realizes that if he were to disinherit him it would benefit instead his new-found son-in-law. Yet all the while Gostanzo remains an amusing old duffer, a malicious fool, perhaps, but a transparent one, easily manipulated because of his blindness to himself. And this is the man who begins the action by persuading his gentle neighbor, Marc Antonio, to trick his son into obedient ways by a show of severity. But his deep plots are not his own, though he thinks they are, for he toils in the web of Rinaldo, a master of duplicity, who drives him deeper and deeper into absurdity—first into accepting his son's own wife into his house and then after being told the truth believing it to be a lie. Irony builds on irony as Gostanzo slogs on in his plots, eventually even forgiving his son in what he takes to be a fine joke on Marc Antonio. He drives himself so furiously in his imagined cleverness that finally Valerio asks, "Gull'd I my father, or gull'd he himself?" (IV.i.206)—a question that was with us from the beginning.

Yet, though it is clear in the main plot, the form of *All Fools* extends through all the parts of the play. It is present, for example, in the title itself, for no one in the play is entirely free from Gostanzo's

6 *All Fools* is technically a *contaminatio*, that is, a mingling of two or more previous plays, just as Terence's *Andria* is based on Menander's Ἀνδρία and Περινθία or Ben Jonson's *The Case is Altered* on Plautus' *Aulularia* and *Captivi*. Chapman took most of the main plot from Terence's *Heautontimoroumenos*, adding to it certain themes from the *Adelphi*. For plot summaries and a full discussion of sources, see Parrott's Introduction.

flaw, and not only in the title, but also in the *Prologus* and Epilogue, where Chapman, in his arrogant manner, pushes beyond the limits of the play to involve the audience itself. They may think themselves superior, judging such plays as his, but they are not allowed to sit easy, for as the *Prologus* tells us, disguised from vulgar ears somewhat in Latin, "*Auriculas asini quis non habet?*" (l. 35). And in the Epilogue the disguise continues, but the intent is the same in the final hesitation that lets the real rhyme strike home:

> We can but bring you meat, and set you stools,
> And to our best cheer say, you all are—welcome.
>
> (ll. 10–11)

What Chapman does for the audience, Valerio reinforces within the play itself in his long, final speech in praise of the "authentical HORN." He extends the essential point of the play, through the metaphor of cuckoldry, to the age at large and all men in it. The world, he says, is a concatenation of fools who are themselves fooled by others. Even poets are not exempt, and at this point Chapman grandiloquently and perhaps honestly includes himself: "For we see the properest men take part of them [cuckold's horns], the best wits cannot avoid them (for then should poets be no cuckolds). Nor can money redeem them, for then would rich men fine for their horns, as they do for offices" (V.ii.314–317). Yet Valerio's speech typically undercuts itself and blunts its own satiric edge since he is drunk when he delivers it, and what he has to say therefore is inflated with drunken exuberance and cannot be taken as the sober truth. But at the same time, the opposite is also true: the drunkenness and the scene in the tavern where the play ends up—young roisterers together with their sober elders, all tricksters tricked—reinforces and supports the truth of his argument.

Another less explicit but more important and more typical expression of the form of the play occurs toward the end of Act II. The first turn of the plot has just succeeded. Valerio has his wife at home, his father is completely gulled, and he feels in a swaggering mood, especially since he has just escaped arrest for debt by dodging through "a troop of lawyers . . ./ Mann'd by their clients" (II.i.324–325). He enters sheathing his sword, and waxing philosophical in his sense of release, he advises the jealous Cornelio to go live at court: "Be a flat courtier, follow some great man,/ Or bring thy wife there, and she'll make thee great" (II.i.356–357). But "clear-eyed" Cornelio

sees it all: "What, to the court? Then take me for a gull" (II.i.358).
And Valerio replies:

> Nay, never shun it to be call'd a gull,
> For I see all the world is but a gull,
> One man gull to another in all kinds.
> A merchant to a courtier is a gull,
> A client to a lawyer is a gull,
> A married man to a bachelor, a gull,
> A bachelor to a cuckold is a gull,
> All to a poet, or a poet to himself.
>
> (II.i.359–366)

After a few lines of generalization, making all the world fools, a chain
of gullers, Valerio settles down to particular examples, which give
the effect of a microcosm. He begins by drawing on his immediate
experiences, which are foremost in his mind—first, his debts in the
merchant-courtier relationship, then the lawyers and clients he has
just run through. These first two examples appear like simple, one-
way gulling operations. The courtier buys costly goods from the
merchant on credit, with no intention of paying for them, just as a
lawyer milks his client by stretching out his case in court for years
with no thought of ending it since the longer he works the more he
gets. But at the same time the gulls foolishly believe that they are in
fact the gullers. The merchant thinks that he is making a killing by
selling expensive, needless fripperies to a court dandy, and the client
hopes eventually to have his fortune made at law through the kind
offices of his lawyer, whom he will use for little pay. At the beginning
of Valerio's speech this sense of reversal is not particularly insistent,
but as the speech proceeds, it emerges more fully. Valerio turns from
himself to Cornelio and picks up the sexual metaphor for gulling that
is used throughout the play. Bachelors gull married men by making
them cuckolds. So much is clear, a fact, perhaps, and a common-
place in Renaissance drama. But then Chapman curiously twists it
backwards in a way that is connected with the form of the play. For
if bachelors gull married men by making them cuckolds, cuckolds
also gull their bachelor gullers by pimping for them, using their
wives to further their own ambitions. Valerio has just told Cornelio
that if he takes his wife to court, she will make him great, and the
same idea is repeated later in Valerio's speech on "the *horned age*":
the cuckold's horn is "A trophy so honorable and unmatchably

powerful that it is able to raise any man from a beggar to an emperor's fellow, a duke's fellow, a nobleman's fellow, alderman's fellow" (V.ii.255–258). And the same form appears more clearly in the last turn of the speech, in which Valerio includes even Chapman himself, who is writing the verse, in his chain of gullers. Again, there is the same sense of reversal, this time swifter than before, for there are no longer two parties involved, but only the poet himself. We have arrived at last at the central, spiritual condition that lies behind the gulling in *All Fools*, having moved steadily in the speech from external, business relationships to the more private, personal concerns of cuckoldry until finally we have come to the self-delusion within the heart of man that underlies them all. For it does not take two to trick a fool. Fools (by which Chapman means all men) gull themselves—poets by their pride, others by their greed, ambition, or desire. And the finest thing is that Valerio's speech is immediately supported and exemplified by the action of the play.

Valerio's swaggering and particularly this speech with its pointed references to cuckoldry offend Cornelio, who despite his jealousy is a man to be reckoned with, and Cornelio sets a trap to catch him:

CORNELIO [*aside*].

    Hark, Dariotto, shall we gull this guller?

DARIOTTO [*aside*].

    He gulls his father, man, we cannot gull him.

                    (II.i.367–368)

But Cornelio proceeds, and again we are treated to the spectacle of a guller gulled by himself. Appealing to Valerio's pride in his recent success and his cultivation of gentlemanly qualities unknown to his father, Cornelio has him play the fool by talking him into cutting a caper for them and singing while accompanying himself on the theorbo only to be deflated in the midst of his performance:

DARIOTTO.

    By heaven, Valerio, and I were thy father,

    And lov'd good qualities as I do my life,

    I'd disinherit thee, for I never heard

    Dog howl with worse grace. . . .

CLAUDIO.

    Call you this touching a theorbo?

OMNES.   Ha, ha, ha!

              Exeunt all but Valerio *and* Rinaldo.

VALERIO.
>How now, what's here?

RINALDO. Zoons, a plot laid to gull thee.
>Could thy wit think the voice was worth the hearing?
>This was the courtier's and the cuckold's project.

(II.i.410–413, 417–420)

And all the while the language supports and extends the action, for everyone speaks of Valerio's imagined accomplishments as *stolen*,[7] that is, secret, assumed on the sly, which is the same word used throughout the play to describe his secret wife.[8] All through the scene we are never allowed to forget the fact that Valerio's humiliation is in some way connected with the gulling of his father. "Nay, that's the very wonder of his wit,/ To carry all without his father's knowledge" (II.i.401–402), Cornelio says at one point. He is speaking, of course, of Valerio's hidden accomplishments, but the language is double and carries us back to Valerio's other success over his father for which this is the inevitable retribution that happens to all fools. "If my father heard me,/ Foot, he'd renounce me for his natural son" (II.i.408–409). He would in either case.

All the characters in the play undergo a similar humiliation in the midst of their finest triumphs. The greatest wit and the most magnificent deceiver of them all is Rinaldo, a natural outsider who has been disappointed in love and thus has no young man's passion to deceive him. He also has nothing to gain since he is a second son and serves therefore in the familiar Jacobean role of the malcontent or in satire the plain dealer, the natural substitute for the tricky slave of classical drama. A scholar of Padua, his only pride and his only enjoyment is in the exercise of his wit. "Fortune, the great commandress of the world," he says,

>Hath divers ways to advance her followers. . . .
>My fortune is to win renown by gulling
>Gostanzo, Dariotto, and Cornelio,
>All which suppose, in all their different kinds,
>Their wits entire, and in themselves no piece.
>All at one blow, my helmet yet unbruis'd,
>I have unhors'd, laid flat on earth for gulls.

(V.i.1–2, 11–16)

[7] II.i.370, 377, 381, 416.
[8] The description of Gratiana in the list of *Actors*, for example, or II.i.6.

This is his greatest moment in the play. Yet all his plots deceive him; his pride and brilliance carry him too far, and shortly afterward everything is laid open by Cornelio, the greatest fool of all. "What a dull slave was I," says Rinaldo eventually, "to be thus gull'd" (V.ii.80). Yet like everyone else in *All Fools* he never changes. His wit and pride remain with him, and immediately after his complete deflation we see him once again in the center of things sprucely setting about to effect the reconciliation.

Dariotto is another example. Although he has the reputation of a stallion who "runn'st through/ The whole town herd, and no man's bed secure" (III.i.275–276), one suspects that he is telling the truth when he says that "the consent,/ Without the act obtain'd, is all I seek./ I love the victory that draws no blood" (III.i.283–285). But even if he is lying, he eventually gets his own and is put out of amorous action for a while by Cornelio, who draws genuine blood in the name of honor. For Dariotto the exquisite world of dalliance became for a moment real, and his fine tricks collapsed: "You'll set a badge on the jealous fool's head, sir. Now set a coxcomb on your own" (III.i.351–352).

Cornelio, in fact, gulls everyone in the play while remaining the most outstanding fool of the lot. And it is in the subplot, centering on Cornelio's distress, that the form of the play is most apparent, for the subplot was Chapman's own. The entire plot is, as it were, an extended metaphor of the action of the main plot. For Cornelio's jealousy and his insane dread of cuckoldry (not to mention cuckoldry itself) are simply another way of seeing a man gulled in more basic, farcical terms. Cornelio is a complete fool. The more he guards his wife and imprisons her in doubt, the more he works against himself and drives her into the arms of Dariotto and all the other courtiers he fears. Yet in the beginning his foolishness is held in stasis. The basic flaw is there, the blindness to himself that makes a fool, but it is not opened or operated on until he gulls Valerio, who then plans to gull him back. All he has to do is whisper that Gazetta is truly unfaithful, and Cornelio is driven mad. He attacks Dariotto and embarks on a divorce. Yet even when he is told the truth, he still believes the lie that bats in his brain: "It may well be. Yet have I cause enough/ To perfect my divorce" (IV.i.367–368). As he sets about on his revenge, the two plots draw together perfectly in the last act, except their positions are now reversed. Cornelio has the upper hand, mirrored, perhaps, by his position on stage, for he probably overlooked the tavern scene and exposed his enemies from the symbolic heights of the upper stage. And this reversal of plots again illustrates in its own medium the basic form of the play. Yet even when the revenge is complete and all the fools are exposed in the tavern for what they are, the fundamental tone that has modified the satire throughout the play remains, full of gusto and good humor. There is no sharpness, no bitterness, no desire to change mankind, only a warm-hearted, large-minded acceptance of our foolish humanity, which makes us more human the dumber and more eccentric we are. In one of the funniest scenes of the play Gostanzo is egged on by Rinaldo to reconcile Cornelio and include him in the happiness of the comedy at the end. Fool calls to fool over abysmal deeps. Gostanzo still fancies himself a Machiavellian who has penetrated the very private parts of wisdom, but his advice to Cornelio is precisely the thing that should most inflame his jealousy. He tells him to imitate his father, who was a cuckold before him: "when he saw ʃtwas but her humor (for his own quietness' sake) he made a back-door to his house for convenience, got a bell to his fore-door, and had an odd fashion in ringing, by which she and her maid knew him, and would stand talking to his next neighbor to prolong time, that all things might be rid cleanly out o' the way before he came, for the credit of his wife. This was wisdom now, for a man's own quiet" (V.ii.196–203). But Cornelio is a fool in his own right and claims that his jealousy was all a deep plot "to bridle . . . [his wife's] stout stomach" (V.ii.213): "I did train the woodcock Dariotto into the net, drew him to my house, gave him opportunity with my wife . . . only to train him in; let him alone with my wife in her bedchamber, and sometimes found him abed with her, and went my way back again softly, only to draw him into the pit" (V.ii.214–220). It sounds almost convincing until at the end the entire spirit of the play peeps through: "And now shall the world see I am as wise as my father" (V.ii.229–230).

THE TEXT

The first references to *All Fools* occur in Henslowe's *Diary* under the working title of "the world Rones A Whelles." They begin on January 22, 1598, and end on July 2, 1599, when Chapman received payment in full.[9] There is no record of its first performance, but it

[9] *Henslowe's Diary*, ed. R. A. Foakes and R. T. Rickert (Cambridge, 1961), pp. 103, 105, 122, 268.

was probably played by the Lord Admiral's Company at The Rose soon after being written. In 1605 it was printed for Thomas Thorpe,[10] who had published his first book, Marston's *Malcontent*, the year before and was later to become famous as the first printer of Shakespeare's *Sonnets*. The title page notes that it was "Presented at the Black *Fryers, And lately before* his Maiestie." According to the *Revels Accounts*, the court performance took place on January 1, 1605.[11] Precisely when it was played at Blackfriars we do not know, nor are we certain that the play as we have it is the same as was written for Henslowe. E. K. Chambers implies that they were two distinct plays, for "the change of company raises a doubt, and there is no 'fool' in *All Fools*."[12] But surely the point of the play is that no fool is necessary since everyone supplies the lack, and most critics believe that the play is the same but that Chapman revised it considerably after joining the Children at Blackfriars. Parrott, for example, Chapman's most important editor, locates the revision primarily "in polishing the verse, in sharpening the dialogue, . . . in heightening the 'humours',", and not in wholesale changes of plot and character.[13] But Parrott has no real reason other than surmise for believing that, and his initial hypothesis that change was necessary to adapt the play to the different stage and audience at Blackfriars.

Without more evidence it is impossible to say anything with confidence, but what few facts we have seem to me to indicate that Chapman did not revise the play as we have it in any thoroughgoing fashion. The *Prologus*, for example, speaks of "those strange effects,/ That rise from this hell, or fall from this heaven" (ll. 3–4). *Heaven* and *hell* refer to the area below the stage and the images of the celestial spheres painted on the shelter above. They were present in an outdoor theater like The Rose, but not at an indoor theater like Blackfriars. If Chapman had revised the play with any care, he would presumably have doctored these lines to fit the change of scene. Again, in the reading of Cornelio's divorce in IV.i.330, the date is given as "the seventeenth of November, fifteen hundred and so

[10] The collation, in a gathering of fours, runs as follows: A_1 blank, A_2 *recto* title page, A_2 *verso* Actors, A_3 *Prologus*, A_4 *recto*—K_1 *recto* All Fooles, K_1 *recto* Epilogue, K_2 blank.

[11] *Extracts from the Accounts of the Revels at Court*, ed. Peter Cunningham, *Shakespeare Society*, XIII (London, 1842), 204.

[12] *The Elizabethan Stage* (Oxford, 1925), III, 252.

[13] Thomas Marc Parrott, ed., *The Comedies of George Chapman* (London, 1914), p. 709.

forth." Since Chapman joined the Children of the Chapel sometime in the year 1600, he would undoubtedly have changed the date in any revision of the play. And finally, the manuscript the printed edition was set from seems to have been the author's own. All the stage directions, for example, are in pompous Latin typical of Chapman's stiff-necked, classical yearnings, not the sort of thing one would expect to find in a promptbook.[14] If, then, the play was printed from Chapman's own manuscript and contains specific allusions to an earlier production at an outdoor theater, it seems reasonable to suppose that it was not revised extensively. Of course that does not mean that Chapman did not revise the play when he joined the Children at Blackfriars, only that the play that survived seems related to a performance in the last year of the sixteenth century. The evidence is thin, perhaps inconsequential, but it is all we have, and it raises almost as many questions as it answers. How could Chapman have carried the manuscript away with him when he left Henslowe, for example, and how did Thorpe get hold of it from Chapman? For Chapman, as we know, was in some difficulties when the play was printed.

After Thorpe's there was no other edition of the play in the seventeenth century, though remainders were apparently bought up by Thomas Dring and resold sometime later on. At the bottom of the list of *Actors* and the bottom of the *Epilogue*, that is, on A_2 *verso* and K_1 *verso*, the following advertisement appears pasted in the Yale copy of the play:

> You may be Furnish'd with most Sorts
> of Plays, at the *White Lion* near
> *Chancery-Lane* end in *Fleet-street*,
> by Thomas Dring.

Dring set up as a stationer in 1649, selling primarily law books and a few plays. He died in 1668, which gives us a range of nineteen years in which copies of *All Fools* were to be purchased once again—just in time for a Restoration revival.

---

14 Evidence of another order is Valerio's long speech in praise of the "authentical HORN" at the end of the play, which is so essentially non-dramatic that it would almost necessarily have been cut in any performance of the play. The fact that it was not cut would seem to support the supposition that what we have here is an edition printed from the author's own manuscript.

Thorpe's text has long been known for its remarkable number of press variants, but these have never been recorded or systematically taken into account in any previous edition. In the collation of the ten copies which form the basis of this text, there were found forty-three errors corrected in press, thirteen of which are substantive. Chases were unlocked and corrections made on the inner forme of A, the inner and outer formes of B, C, D, E, G, and I, and the inner forme of K. The substantive variants are recorded in the textual notes.

The text of the present edition is based on a collation of ten copies of the 1605 quarto: Yale University, Harvard University, Edinburgh University, The Boston Public Library, The Folger Shakespeare Library, The Pierpont Morgan Library, The Bodleian, The University of Texas (two copies), and The Henry E. Huntington Library. These represent more than fifty percent of the copies that survive.[15]

FRANK MANLEY

Emory University

[15] I should like to thank the Research Fund of Emory University for assistance in preparing this edition.

ALL FOOLS

ACTORS

GOSTANZO ⎱ knights
MARC ANTONIO ⎰

VALERIO, *son to Gostanzo*

FORTUNIO, *elder son to Marc Antonio*   5

RINALDO, *the younger*

DARIOTTO ⎱ *courtiers*
CLAUDIO ⎰

CORNELIO, *a start-up gentleman*   10

CURIO, *a page*

KYTE, *a scrivener*

FRANCIS POCK, *a surgeon*

[DRAWERS]

GAZETTA, *wife to Cornelio*   15

BELLANORA, *daughter to Gostanzo*

GRATIANA, *stolen wife to Valerio*

---

6. *Rinaldo*] also spelled "Rynaldo" in the original quarto, calling to mind his fox-like qualities. See also I.i. 92–93.

10. *Cornelio*] Latin *cornus* or *horn*; therefore, a cuckold.

10. *start-up*] an upstart, parvenu.

12. *Kyte*] "kite" or buzzard.

13. *Pock*] "pox" or syphilis.

17. *stolen*] secret.

PROLOGUS

The fortune of a stage (like Fortune's self)
Amazeth greatest judgments, and none knows
The hidden causes of those strange effects,
That rise from this hell, or fall from this heaven.
Who can show cause why your wits, that in aim   5
At higher objects, scorn to compose plays
(Though we are sure they could, would they vouchsafe it!),
Should (without means to make) judge better far,
Than those that make? And yet ye see they can.
For without your applause wretched is he   10
That undertakes the stage, and he's more blest
That with your glorious favors can contest.
Who can show cause why th'ancient comic vein
Of Eupolis and Cratinus (now reviv'd,
Subject to personal application)   15
Should be exploded by some bitter spleens,
Yet merely comical and harmless jests
(Though ne'er so witty) be esteem'd but toys,
If void of th'other satirism's sauce?
Who can show cause why quick Venerian jests   20
Should sometimes ravish, sometimes fall far short
Of the just length and pleasure of your ears,
When our pure dames think them much less obscene
Than those that win your panegyric spleen?
But our poor dooms (alas) you know are nothing.   25
To your inspired censure ever we

---

4. *this hell . . . this heaven*] the area below the stage (the *hell*) and the shelter above the platform, often painted with images of the celestial spheres (the *heavens*).

14. *Eupolis and Cratinus*] contemporaries of Aristophanes and next to him the two greatest writers of Greek Old Comedy.

16. *bitter spleens*] ill-humored persons.

22. *length*] reach, i.e., earshot.

24. *panegyric spleen*] fits of praise. The spleen was regarded as the seat of various emotions, and it is difficult to say precisely what it means in a particular context without some qualifying word to explain it, as here, or at l. 16.

25. *dooms*] judgments.

Must needs submit, and there's the mystery.
  Great are the gifts given to united heads,
To gifts, attire, to fair attire, the stage
Helps much. For if our other audience see   30
You on the stage depart before we end,
Our wits go with you all, and we are fools.
So Fortune governs in these stage events,
That merit bears least sway in most contents.
Auriculas asini quis non habet?   35
How we shall then appear, we must refer
To magic of your dooms, that never err.

27. mystery] *Q* (*corr.*); misery *Q*
(*uncorr.*).

28–32. *Great . . . fools*] Chapman directs his satire against the rich young men of the time who paid extra to sit on the stage in order to see and be seen.

28. *united heads*] a number of heads put together, as in an audience.

30. *other audience*] the audience in the theater proper, as opposed to those sitting on the stage.

34. *contents*] the satisfaction or pleasure of the audience.

35. *Auriculas . . . habet?*] "Who doesn't have ass's ears?" (Persius, *Satire* I, 121).

ALL FOOLS

[I.i]   *Enter* Rinaldo, Fortunio, Valerio.

RINALDO.

    Can one self cause, in subjects so alike
    As you two are, produce effects so unlike?
    One like the turtle, all in mournful strains
    Wailing his fortunes, th'other like the lark,
    Mounting the sky in shrill and cheerful notes,   5
    Chanting his joys aspir'd. And both for love.
    In one, love raiseth by his violent heat
    Moist vapors from the heart into the eyes,
    From whence they drown his breast in daily showers.
    In th'other, his divided power infuseth   10
    Only a temperate and most kindly warmth,
    That gives life to those fruits of wit and virtue,
    Which the unkind hand of an uncivil father
    Had almost nipp'd in the delightsome blossom.

FORTUNIO.

    O, brother, love rewards our services   15
    With a most partial and injurious hand,
    If you consider well our different fortunes.
    Valerio loves, and joys the dame he loves.
    I love, and never can enjoy the sight
    Of her I love, so far from conquering   20
    In my desire's assault, that I can come
    To lay no batt'ry to the fort I seek,
    All passages to it so strongly kept
    By strait guard of her father.

1. subjects] *Q* (*corr.*); subject *Q*   3. strains] *Q* (*corr.*); steaines *Q*
(*uncorr.*).   (*uncorr.*).
2. effects] *Q* (*corr.*); effect *Q*
(*uncorr.*).

3. *turtle*] turtledove.

RINALDO.   I dare swear,
  If just desert in love measur'd reward,   25
  Your fortune should exceed Valerio's far.
  For I am witness (being your bedfellow)
  Both to the daily and the nightly service
  You do unto the deity of love,
  In vows, sighs, tears, and solitary watches.   30
  He never serves him with such sacrifice,
  Yet hath his bow and shafts at his command.
  Love's service is much like our humorous lords';
  Where minions carry more than servitors,
  The bold and careless servant still obtains;   35
  The modest and respective, nothing gains.
  You never see your love, unless in dreams,
  He, Hymen puts in whole possession.
  What different stars reign'd when your loves were born,
  He forc'd to wear the willow, you the horn?   40
  But, brother, are you not asham'd to make
  Yourself a slave to the base lord of love,
  Begot of Fancy, and of Beauty born?
  And what is Beauty? A mere quintessence,
  Whose life is not in being, but in seeming,   45
  And therefore is not to all eyes the same,
  But like a cozening picture, which one way
  Shows like a crow, another like a swan.
  And upon what ground is this Beauty drawn?
  Upon a woman, a most brittle creature,   50
  And would to God (for my part) that were all.
FORTUNIO.
    But tell me, brother, did you never love?
RINALDO.
    You know I did, and was belov'd again,
    And that of such a dame as all men deem'd

---

31. *He*] i.e., Valerio.
33. *humorous*] whimsical, capricious.
34. *carry*] have more influence.
35. *still obtains*] always prospers.
36. *respective*] attentive, careful.
38. *Hymen*] god of marriage.
40. *willow . . . horn*] Signs of the deserted lover and of cuckoldry.
47. *cozening*] deceiving.

Honor'd, and made me happy in her favors. 55
Exceeding fair she was not, and yet fair
In that she never studied to be fairer
Than Nature made her. Beauty cost her nothing.
Her virtues were so rare, they would have made
An Ethiop beautiful, at least so thought 60
By such as stood aloof, and did observe her
With credulous eyes. But what they were indeed
I'll spare to blaze, because I lov'd her once.
Only I found her such, as for her sake
I vow eternal wars against their whole sex. 65
Inconstant shuttlecocks, loving fools, and jesters,
Men rich in dirt and titles, sooner won
With the most vile than the most virtuous,
Found true to none. If one amongst whole hundreds
Chance to be chaste, she is so proud withal, 70
Wayward and rude, that one of unchaste life
Is oftentimes approv'd a worthier wife.
Undressed, sluttish, nasty to their husbands,
Spong'd up, adorn'd, and painted to their lovers.
All day in ceaseless uproar with their households, 75
If all the night their husbands have not pleas'd them.
Like hounds, most kind, being beaten and abus'd,
Like wolves, most cruel, being kindliest us'd.

FORTUNIO.

Fie, thou profan'st the deity of their sex.

RINALDO.

Brother, I read that Egypt heretofore 80
Had temples of the richest frame on earth,
Much like this goodly edifice of women.
With alabaster pillars were those temples
Upheld and beautified, and so are women.
Most curiously glaz'd, and so are women. 85
Cunningly painted too, and so are women.
In outside wondrous heavenly, so are women.
But when a stranger view'd those fanes within,

81. richest] *Dodsley*; riches *Q*.

---

74. *Spong'd up*] made spruce or trim.
88. *fanes*] temples.

Instead of gods and goddesses, he should find
A painted fowl, a fury, or a serpent,   90
And such celestial inner parts have women.
VALERIO.
Rinaldo, the poor fox that lost his tail,
Persuaded others also to lose theirs.
Thyself, for one perhaps that for desert
Or some defect in thy attempts refus'd thee,   95
Revil'st the whole sex, beauty, love, and all.
I tell thee love is nature's second sun,
Causing a spring of virtues where he shines.
And as without the sun, the world's great eye,
All colors, beauties, both of art and nature,   100
Are given in vain to men, so without love
All beauties bred in women are in vain,
All virtues born in men lie buried.
For love informs them as the sun doth colors.
And as the sun, reflecting his warm beams   105
Against the earth, begets all fruits and flowers,
So love, fair shining in the inward man,
Brings forth in him the honorable fruits
Of valor, wit, virtue, and haughty thoughts,
Brave resolution, and divine discourse.   110
O, 'tis the Paradise, the Heaven of earth.
And didst thou know the comfort of two hearts
In one delicious harmony united,
As to joy one joy, and think both one thought,
Live both one life, and therein double life,   115
To see their souls met at an interview
In their bright eyes, at parley in their lips,
Their language kisses, and t'observe the rest,
Touches, embraces, and each circumstance
Of all love's most unmatched ceremonies,   120
Thou wouldst abhor thy tongue for blasphemy.
O, who can comprehend how sweet love tastes
But he that hath been present at his feasts?

97. sun] *Parrott*; sonne *Q*.

---

92. *the poor fox*] one of Aesop's fables. The fox had lost his tail in a trap, but according to Aesop, he was not able to persuade the others to give up theirs.

RINALDO.

> Are you in that vein too, Valerio?
> 'Twere fitter you should be about your charge,   125
> How plow and cart goes foward. I have known
> Your joys were all employ'd in husbandry.
> Your study was how many loads of hay
> A meadow of so many acres yielded,
> How many oxen such a close would fat.   130
> And is your rural service now converted
> From Pan to Cupid, and from beasts to women?
> O, if your father knew this, what a lecture
> Of bitter castigation he would read you!

VALERIO.

> My father? Why my father? Does he think   135
> To rob me of myself? I hope I know
> I am a gentleman. Though his covetous humor
> And education hath transform'd me bailie,
> And made me overseer of his pastures,
> I'll be myself, in spite of husbandry.   140

> > *Enter* Gratiana.

> And see, bright heaven, here comes my husbandry.

> > *Amplectitur eam.*

> Here shall my cattle graze, here nectar drink,
> Here will I hedge and ditch, here hide my treasure.
> O poor Fortunio, how wouldst thou triumph,
> If thou enjoy'dst this happiness with my sister!   145

FORTUNIO.

> I were in heaven if once 'twere come to that.

RINALDO.

> And methinks 'tis my heaven that I am past it.
> And should the wretched Machiavellian,
> The covetous knight, your father, see this sight,

---

127. *husbandry*] farming, but also a pun, since Valerio is secretly married. The word is often used in the play in this double sense.

130. *close*] pasture.

138. *bailie*] overseer of an estate.

141.1. *Amplectitur eam*] embraces her.

148. *Machiavellian*] not politically (though Gostanzo is constantly called *politic*, referring to his Machiavellian nature), but morally. Like most Machiavellians, Gostanzo is totally unscrupulous.

Lusty Valerio?

VALERIO.   'Sfoot, sir, if he should,   150
He shall perceive ere long my skill extends
To something more than sweaty husbandry.

RINALDO.

I'll bear thee witness, thou canst skill of dice,
Cards, tennis, wenching, dancing, and what not,
And this is something more than husbandry!   155
Th'art known in ordinaries, and tobacco shops,
Trusted in taverns and in vaulting houses,
And this is something more than husbandry.
Yet all this while, thy father apprehends thee
For the most tame and thrifty groom in Europe.   160

FORTUNIO.

Well, he hath ventur'd on a marriage
Would quite undo him, did his father know it.

RINALDO.

Know it? Alas sir, where can he bestow
This poor gentlewoman he hath made his wife,
But his inquisitive father will hear of it,   165
Who, like the dragon to th' Hesperian fruit,
Is to his haunts? 'Slight! Hence, the old knight comes.

        Intrat Gostanzo. *Omnes aufugiunt.*

GOSTANZO.

Rinaldo.

RINALDO.   Who's that calls? What, Sir Gostanzo?
How fares your knighthood, sir?

GOSTANZO.   Say, who was that
Shrunk at my entry here? Was't not your brother?   170

RINALDO.

He shrunk not, sir. His business call'd him hence.

---

150. *'Sfoot*] God's foot, a mild oath.
153. *canst skill*] know something about.
156. *ordinaries*] eating houses or the public rooms at inns where meals
were provided at a fixed price.
157. *vaulting houses*] whore houses.
166. *dragon . . . fruit*] the dragon Ladon, who guarded the golden apples
of the Hesperides. It had many heads and never slept.
167. *'Slight*] God's light.
167.1. *Intrat . . . aufugiunt*] Enter Gostanzo. Everybody runs away.

GOSTANZO.

And was it not my son that went out with him?

RINALDO.

I saw not him. I was in serious speech
About a secret business with my brother.

GOSTANZO.

Sure 'twas my son. What made he here? I sent him   175
About affairs to be dispatch'd in haste.

RINALDO.

Well, sir, lest silence breed unjust suspect,
I'll tell a secret I am sworn to keep,
And crave your honored assistance in it.

GOSTANZO.

What is't, Rinaldo?

RINALDO.   This, sir: 'twas your son.   180

GOSTANZO.

And what young gentlewoman grac'd their company?

RINALDO.

Thereon depends the secret I must utter.
That gentlewoman hath my brother married.

GOSTANZO.

Married? What is she?

RINALDO.   'Faith, sir, a gentlewoman,
But her unnourishing dowry must be told   185
Out of her beauty.

GOSTANZO.   Is it true, Rinaldo?
And does your father understand so much?

RINALDO.

That was the motion, sir, I was entreating
Your son to make to him, because I know
He is well spoken and may much prevail   190
In satisfying my father, who much loves him,
Both for his wisdom and his husbandry.

GOSTANZO.

Indeed he's one can tell his tale, I tell you,
And for his husbandry—

RINALDO.   O, sir, had you heard

185. unnourishing] Q (*corr.*); un-
usering Q (*uncorr.*).

What thrifty discipline he gave my brother   195
For making choice without my father's knowledge
And without riches, you would have admir'd him.
GOSTANZO.
Nay, nay, I know him well. But what was it?
RINALDO.
That in the choice of wives men must respect
The chief wife, riches, that in every course   200
A man's chief lodestar should shine out of riches,
Love nothing heartily in this world but riches,
Cast off all friends, all studies, all delights,
All honesty, and religion for riches,
And many such, which wisdom sure he learn'd   205
Of his experient father. Yet my brother
So soothes his rash affection, and presumes
So highly on my father's gentle nature,
That he's resolv'd to bring her home to him,
And like enough he will.
GOSTANZO.   And like enough   210
Your silly father, too, will put it up.
An honest knight, but much too much indulgent
To his presuming children.
RINALDO.   What a difference
Doth interpose itself 'twixt him and you!
Had your son us'd you thus!
GOSTANZO.   My son? Alas,   215
I hope to bring him up in other fashion.
Follows my husbandry, sets early foot
Into the world. He comes not at the city,
Nor knows the city arts.
RINALDO.   But dice and wenching.   *Aversus.*
GOSTANZO.
Acquaints himself with no delight but getting,   220
A perfect pattern of sobriety,
Temperance, and husbandry to all my household.
And what's his company, I pray? Not wenches.

---

195. *thrifty discipline*] sensible chastisement or correction.
219. *S.D. Aversus*] aside.

RINALDO.

Wenches? I durst be sworn he never smelt
A wench's breath yet. But methinks 'twere fit   225
You sought him out a wife.

GOSTANZO.   A wife, Rinaldo?

He dares not look a woman in the face.

RINALDO.

'Sfoot, hold him to one. Your son such a sheep?

GOSTANZO.

'Tis strange, in earnest.

RINALDO.

Well, sir, though for my thriftless brother's sake,   230
I little care how my wrong'd father takes it,
Yet for my father's quiet, if yourself
Would join hands with your wise and toward son,
I should deserve it some way.

GOSTANZO.   Good Rinaldo,

I love you and your father, but this matter   235
Is not for me to deal in. And 'tis needless.
You say your brother is resolv'd, presuming
Your father will allow it.

Enter Marc Antonio.

RINALDO.   See, my father.

Since you are resolute not to move him, sir,
In any case conceal the secret by way   *Abscondit se.* 240
Of an atonement. Let me pray you will.

GOSTANZO.

Upon mine honor.

RINALDO.   Thanks, sir.

MARC ANTONIO.

God save thee, honorable Knight Gostanzo.

GOSTANZO.

Friend Marc Antonio? Welcome. And I think
I have good news to welcome you withal.   245

RINALDO [*aside*].

He cannot hold.

233. wise] *Shepherd*; wife *Q*.

---

233. *toward*] "making good progress in learning or practice" (*OED*).
240. *S.D. Abscondit se*] Hides himself.
246. *hold*] keep it to himself.

MARC ANTONIO.   What news, I pray you, sir?
GOSTANZO.
    You have a forward, valiant, eldest son,
    But wherein is his forwardness and valor?
MARC ANTONIO.
    I know not wherein you intend him so.
GOSTANZO.
    Forward before, valiant behind, his duty,   250
    That he hath dar'd before your due consent
    To take a wife.
MARC ANTONIO.   A wife, sir? What is she?
GOSTANZO.
    One that is rich enough: her hair pure amber,
    Her forehead mother of pearl, her fair eyes
    Two wealthy diamonds, her lips mines of rubies.   255
    Her teeth are orient pearl, her neck pure ivory.
MARC ANTONIO.
    Jest not, good sir, in an affair so serious.
    I love my son, and if his youth reward me
    With his contempt of my consent in marriage,
    'Tis to be fear'd that his presumption builds not   260
    Of his good choice, that will bear out itself,
    And being bad, the news is worse than bad.
GOSTANZO.
    What call you bad? Is it bad to be poor?
MARC ANTONIO.
    The world accounts it so. But if my son
    Have in her birth and virtues held his choice   265
    Without disparagement, the fault is less.
GOSTANZO.
    Sits the wind there? Blows there so calm a gale
    From a contemned and deserved anger?
    Are you so easy to be disobey'd?

264. son] *Collier*; soone *Q*.

---

249. *intend*] think, judge.
260–261.] "''Tis to be feared that his over-confident conduct is not
grounded upon the goodness of his choice which would warrant his action"
(Parrott).
266. *disparagement*] dishonor and disgrace of marriage to one of inferior
rank.

MARC ANTONIO.

What should I do? If my enamor'd son   270
Have been so forward, I assure myself
He did it more to satisfy his love
Than to incense my hate, or to neglect me.

GOSTANZO.

A passing kind construction. Suffer this,
You ope him doors to any villainy.   275
He'll dare to sell, to pawn, run ever riot,
Despise your love in all, and laugh at you.
And that knight's competency you have gotten
With care and labor, he with lust and idleness
Will bring into the stipend of a beggar,   280
All to maintain a wanton whirligig,
Worth nothing more than she brings on her back.
Yet all your wealth too little for that back.
By heaven, I pity your declining state,
For be assur'd your son hath set his foot   285
In the right pathway to consumption:
Up to the heart in love, and for that love
Nothing can be too dear his love desires.
And how insatiate and unlimited
Is the ambition and the beggarly pride   290
Of a dame hoised from a beggar's state
To a state competent and plentiful,
You cannot be so simple not to know.

MARC ANTONIO.

I must confess the mischief, but, alas,
Where is in me the power of remedy?   295

GOSTANZO.

Where? In your just displeasure. Cast him off.
Receive him not. Let him endure the use
Of their enforced kindness that must trust him

---

274. *passing*] surpassing.
278. *knight's competency*] income suitable to a knight.
280. *stipend*] income.
291. *hoised*] raised aloft, as with a block and tackle.
294–295. *mischief . . . remedy*] legal terms. In Renaissance law a mischief was "a condition in which a person suffers a wrong or is under some disability, *esp.* one for which equity affords a remedy" (*OED*).

For meat and money, for apparel, house,
And everything belongs to that estate,   300
Which he must learn with want of misery,
Since pleasure and a full estate hath blinded
His dissolute desires.
MARC ANTONIO.   What should I do?
If I should banish him my house and sight,
What desperate resolution might it breed   305
To run into the wars, and there to live
In want of competency and perhaps
Taste th'unrecoverable loss of his chief limbs,   ⟨
Which while he hath in peace, at home with me,
May, with his spirit, ransom his estate   310
From any loss his marriage can procure.
GOSTANZO.
Is't true? Nay, let him run into the war,
And lose what limbs he can. Better one branch
Be lopp'd away, than all the whole tree should perish,
And for his wants, better young want than old.   315
You have a younger son at Padua.
I like his learning well. Make him your heir,
And let your other walk. Let him buy wit
At's own charge, not at's father's. If you lose him,
You lose no more than that was lost before.   320
If you recover him, you find a son.
MARC ANTONIO.
I cannot part with him.
GOSTANZO.   If it be so,
And that your love to him be so extreme,
In needful dangers ever choose the least.
If he should be in mind to pass the seas,   325
Your son Rinaldo (who told me all this)
Will tell me that, and so we shall prevent it.
If by no stern course you will venture that,

312. Nay] *Parrott*; Ne *Q*.

---

301. *want of misery*] the misery of poverty.
315. *better . . . old*] variant of the proverb "an idle youth, a needy age."
See Tilley, Y 38.
316. *Padua*] the university of Padua, founded in the thirteenth century
and renowned in Elizabethan England for its learning.

Let him come home to me with his fair wife,
And if you chance to see him, shake him up,   330
As if your wrath were hard to be reflected,
That he may fear hereafter to offend
In other dissolute courses. At my house,
With my advice and my son's good example,
Who shall serve as a glass for him to see   335
His faults, and mend them to his precedent,
I make no doubt but of a dissolute son
And disobedient, to send him home
Both dutiful and thrifty.
MARC ANTONIO.   O, Gostanzo!
Could you do this, you should preserve yourself   340
A perfect friend of me, and me a son.
GOSTANZO.
Remember you your part, and fear not mine.
Rate him, revile him, and renounce him too.
Speak, can you do't, man?
MARC ANTONIO.   I'll do all I can.
                              Exit Marc Antonio.
GOSTANZO.
Alas, good man, how nature overweighs him.   345

                    Rinaldo *comes forth.*

RINALDO.
God save you, sir.
GOSTANZO.   Rinaldo, all the news
You told me as a secret, I perceive
Is passing common, for your father knows it.
The first thing he related was the marriage.
RINALDO.
And was extremely mov'd?
GOSTANZO.   Beyond all measure.   350

342. mine] *Q* (*corr.*); wine *Q*
(*uncorr.*).

---

331. *reflected*] appeased, with some carry over of the root meaning,
"to turn" or "bend back."
335. *glass*] mirror.

But I did all I could to quench his fury,
Told him how easy 'twas for a young man
To run that amorous course, and though his choice
Were nothing rich, yet she was gently born,
Well qualified and beautiful. But he still   355
Was quite relentless, and would needs renounce him.
RINALDO.
My brother knows it well, and is resolv'd
To trail a pike in field, rather than bide
The more fear'd push of my vex'd father's fury.
GOSTANZO.
Indeed that's one way. But are no more means   360
Left to his fine wits than t'incense his father
With a more violent rage, and to redeem
A great offense with greater?
RINALDO.   So I told him,
But to a desperate mind all breath is lost.
GOSTANZO.
Go to, let him be wise, and use his friends,   365
Amongst whom I'll be foremost, to his father.
Without this desperate error he intends
Join'd to the other, I'll not doubt to make him
Easy return into his father's favor,
So he submit himself, as duty binds him.   370
For fathers will be known to be themselves,
And often when their angers are not deep
Will paint an outward rage upon their looks.
RINALDO.
All this I told him, sir. But what says he?
"I know my father will not be reclaim'd.   375
He'll think that if he wink at this offense,
'Twill open doors to any villainy.
I'll dare to sell, to pawn, and run all riot,
To laugh at all his patience, and consume
All he hath purchas'd to an honor'd purpose   380
In maintenance of a wanton whirligig
Worth nothing more than she wears on her back."

---

359. *push*] attack.

GOSTANZO [*aside*].

    The very words I us'd t'incense his father.—
    But, good Rinaldo, let him be advis'd.
    How would his father grieve, should he be maim'd,   385
    Or quite miscarry in the ruthless war!

RINALDO.

    I told him so. But, "Better far," said he,
    "One branch should utterly be lopp'd away,
    Than the whole tree of all his race should perish;
    And for his wants, better young want than eld."   390

GOSTANZO [*aside*].

    By heaven, the same words still I us'd t'his father.
    Why comes this about? —Well, good Rinaldo,
    If he dare not endure his father's looks,
    Let him and his fair wife come home to me,
    Till I have qualified his father's passion.   395
    He shall be kindly welcome and be sure
    Of all the intercession I can use.

RINALDO.

    I thank you, sir. I'll try what I can do,
    Although I fear me I shall strive in vain.

GOSTANZO.

    Well, try him, try him.   *Exit.*

RINALDO.   Thanks, sir, so I will.—   400
    See, this old, politic, dissembling knight,
    Now he perceives my father so affectionate,
    And that my brother may hereafter live
    By him and his with equal use of either,
    He will put on a face of hollow friendship.   405
    But this will prove an excellent ground to sow
    The seed of mirth amongst us. I'll go seek
    Valerio and my brother, and tell them
    Such news of their affairs as they'll admire.   *Exit.*

[I.ii]   *Enter* Gazetta, Bellanora, Gratiana.

GAZETTA.

    How happy are your fortunes above mine!

---

390. *eld*] old age.

Both still being woo'd and courted, still so feeding
On the delights of love that still you find
An appetite to more, where I am cloy'd,
And being bound to love-sports, care not for them.   5

BELLANORA.

That is your fault, Gazetta. We have loves
And wish continual company with them
In honor'd marriage-rites, which you enjoy.
But seld or never can we get a look
Of those we love. Fortunio, my dear choice,   10
Dare not be known to love me, nor come near
My father's house, where I as in a prison
Consume my lost days and the tedious nights,
My father guarding me for one I hate.
And Gratiana here, my brother's love,   15
Joys him by so much stealth that vehement fear
Drinks up the sweetness of their stol'n delights,
Where you enjoy a husband, and may freely
Perform all obsequies you desire to love.

GAZETTA.

Indeed I have a husband, and his love   20
Is more than I desire, being vainly jealous.
Extremes, though contrary, have the like effects.
Extreme heat mortifies like extreme cold;
Extreme love breeds satiety as well
As extreme hatred, and too violent rigor   25
Tempts chastity as much as too much licence.
There's no man's eye fix'd on me but doth pierce
My husband's soul. If any ask my welfare,
He straight doubts treason practic'd to his bed,
Fancies but to himself all likelihoods   30
Of my wrong to him, and lays all on me
For certain truths. Yet seeks he with his best
To put disguise on all his jealousy,

23. Extreme heat] *Dodsley*; Extremes heate *Q*.

---

9. *seld*] seldom.
23. *mortifies*] kills.
29. *doubts*] suspects.

Fearing perhaps lest it may teach me that
Which otherwise I should not dream upon.   35
Yet lives he still abroad at great expense,
Turns merely gallant from his farmer's state,
Uses all games and recreations,
Runs races with the gallants of the court,
Feasts them at home, and entertains them costly.   40
And then upbraids me with their company.

Enter Cornelio.

See, see, we shall be troubled with him now.
CORNELIO.
Now, ladies, what plots have we now in hand?
They say when only one dame is alone
She plots some mischief, but if three together,   45
They plot three hundred. Wife, the air is sharp.
Y'ad best to take the house lest you take cold.
GAZETTA.
Alas, this time of year yields no such danger.
CORNELIO.
Go in, I say. A friend of yours attends you.
GAZETTA.
He is of your bringing, and may stay.   50
CORNELIO.
Nay, stand not chopping logic. In, I pray.
GAZETTA.
Ye see, gentlewomen, what my happiness is.
These humors reign in marriage. Humors, humors.
                        Exit [Gazetta]. *He followeth.*
GRATIANA.
Now by my sooth, I am no fortune-teller,
And would be loath to prove so, yet pronounce   55
This at adventure, that 'twere indecorum
This heifer should want horns.
BELLANORA.   Fie on this love.
I rather wish to want than purchase so.

---

42. we] *Q (corr.)*; wee, wee *Q*
(uncorr.).

37. *merely*] completely.

GRATIANA.

    Indeed such love is like a smoky fire
    In a cold morning. Though the fire be cheerful,   60
    Yet is the smoke so sour and cumbersome,
    'Twere better lose the fire than find the smoke.
    Such an attendant then as smoke to fire
    Is jealousy to love. Better want both
    Than have both.

                    Enter Valerio *and* Fortunio.

VALERIO.   Come, Fortunio, now take hold   65
    On this occasion, as myself on this.   [*Embraces* Gratiana.]
    One couple more would make a barley-break.

FORTUNIO.

    I fear, Valerio, we shall break too soon.
    Your father's jealous spy-all will displease us.

VALERIO.

    Well, wench, the day will come his Argus eyes   70
    Will shut, and thou shalt open. 'Sfoot, I think
    Dame Nature's memory begins to fail her.
    If I write but my name in mercers' books,
    I am as sure to have at six months' end
    A rascal at my elbow with his mace,   75
    As I am sure my father's not far hence.
    My father yet hath ought Dame Nature debt
    These threescore years and ten, yet calls not on him.
    But if she turn her debt-book over once,
    And finding him her debtor, do but send   80
    Her sergeant, John Death, to arrest his body,

69. jealous] *Shepherd*; Ielosie *Q.*

---

    67. *barley-break*] country game played by three couples, usually in a
field of grain. When hard pressed by the "catchers," a couple was allowed
to separate or "break."
    73. *mercers' books*] "Proverbial in the Elizabethan period with reference
to the debts of a gallant" (*OED*). A mercer was a clothes merchant who
dealt in expensive material such as silk and velvet.
    75. *rascal . . . mace*] bailiff or deputy sheriff with his staff of authority.
    77. *ought*] owed.
    78.] The subject of *calls* is *Nature* in l. 77.
    81. *sergeant*] officer of a court responsible for making arrests.

Our souls shall rest, wench, then, and the free light
Shall triumph in our faces, where now night,
In imitation of my father's frowns,
Lowers at our meeting.

Enter Rinaldo.

See where the scholar comes.   85

RINALDO.

Down on your knees, poor lovers. Reverence learning.

FORTUNIO.

I pray thee, why, Rinaldo?

RINALDO.   Mark what cause
Flows from my depth of knowledge to your loves,
To make you kneel and bless me while you live.

VALERIO.

I pray thee, good scholard, give us cause.   90

RINALDO.

Mark then, erect your ears. —[*To* Valerio.]   You know
    what horror
Would fly on your love from your father's frowns,
If he should know it. And your sister here
(My brother's sweetheart) knows as well what rage
Would seize his powers for her, if he should know   95
My brother woo'd her, or that she lov'd him.
Is not this true? Speak all.

OMNES.   All this is true.

RINALDO.

It is as true that now you meet by stealth
In depth of midnight, kissing out at grates,
Climb over walls. And all this I'll reform.   100

VALERIO.

By logic.

RINALDO.   Well, sir, you shall have all means
To live in one house, eat and drink together,
Meet and kiss your fills.

VALERIO.   All this by learning?

RINALDO.

Ay, and your frowning father know all this.

90. *scholard*] scholar.
95. *seize . . . her*] come over him towards her.

VALERIO.

    Ay, marry, small learning may prove that.   105

RINALDO.

    Nay, he shall know it, and desire it too,

    Welcome my brother to him, and your wife,

    Entreating both to come and dwell with him.

    Is not this strange?

FORTUNIO.   Ay, too strange to be true.

RINALDO.

    'Tis in this head shall work it. Therefore, hear.   110

    Brother, this lady you must call your wife,

    For I have told her sweetheart's father here

    That she is your wife. And because my father

    (Who now believes it) must be quieted

    Before you see him, you must live awhile   115

    As husband to her in his father's house.

    Valerio, here's a simple mean for you

    To lie at rack and manger with your wedlock,

    And, brother, for yourself to meet as freely

    With this your long-desir'd and barred love.   120

FORTUNIO.

    You make us wonder.

RINALDO.   Peace, be rul'd by me,

    And you shall see to what a perfect shape

    I'll bring this rude plot, which blind Chance (the ape

    Of counsel and advice) hath brought forth blind.

    Valerio, can your heat of love forbear   125

    Before your father, and allow my brother

    To use some kindness to your wife before him?

VALERIO.

    Ay, before him I do not greatly care,

    Nor anywhere indeed. My sister here

    Shall be my spy. If she will wrong herself,   130

    And give her right to my wife, I am pleas'd.

FORTUNIO.

    My dearest life I know will never fear

113. wife] _Q_ (_corr._); wifs _Q_ (_un-
corr._).

---

118. _lie . . . manger_] live in plenty.

Any such will or thought in all my powers.
When I court her then, think I think 'tis thee,
When I embrace her, hold thee in mine arms.   135
Come, let us practice gainst we see your father.
                              [*Offers to embrace* Gratiana.]
VALERIO.
    Soft, sir, I hope you need not do it yet.
    Let me take this time.   [*Embraces her.*]
RINALDO.   Come, you must not touch her.
VALERIO.
    No, not before my father!
RINALDO.   No, nor now,
    Because you are so soon to practice it,   140
    For I must bring them to him presently.
    Take her, Fortunio. Go hence man and wife.
    We will attend you rarely with fix'd faces.
    Valerio, keep your countenance, and conceive
    Your father in your forged sheepishness,   145
    Who thinks thou dar'st not look upon a wench,
    Nor knowest at which end to begin to kiss her.   *Exeunt.*

                    Finis Actus Primi.

[II.i]   Gostanzo, Marc Antonio.

GOSTANZO.
    It is your own too simple lenity
    And doting indulgence shown to him still
    That thus hath taught your son to be no son.
    As you have us'd him, therefore, so you have him.
    Durst my son thus turn rebel to his duty,   5
    Steal up a match unsuiting his estate,
    Without all knowledge of or friend or father,
    And to make that good with a worse offense,

6. unsuiting] *Parrott*; unshuting *Q*.

---

136. *gainst*] in preparation for the time when.
143. *rarely*] remarkably well, splendidly.
144–145. *conceive . . . father*] make your father conceive of.
[II.i]
    7. *or . . . or*] either . . . or.

Resolve to run beyond sea to the wars,
Durst my son serve me thus? Well, I have stay'd him,   10
Though much against my disposition,
And this hour I have set for his repair
With his young mistress and concealed wife,
And in my house here they shall sojourn both,
Till your black anger's storm be overblown.   15

MARC ANTONIO.

My anger's storm? Ah, poor Fortunio,
One gentle word from thee would soon resolve
The storm of my rage to a shower of tears.

GOSTANZO.

In that vein still? Well, Marc Antonio,
Our old acquaintance and long neighborhood   20
Ties my affection to you and the good
Of your whole house; in kind regard whereof
I have advis'd you for your credit sake,
And for the tender welfare of your son,
To frown on him a little. If you do not,   25
But at first parley take him to your favor,
I protest utterly to renounce all care
Of you and yours and all your amities.
They say he's wretched that out of himself
Cannot draw counsel to his proper weal.   30
But he's thrice wretched that has neither counsel
Within himself, nor apprehension
Of counsel for his own good from another.

MARC ANTONIO.

Well, I will arm myself against this weakness
The best I can. I long to see this Helen   35
That hath enchanted my young Paris thus,
And's like to set all our poor Troy on fire.

Enter Valerio *with a* Page.

GOSTANZO.

Here comes my son. Withdraw, take up your stand.

9. Resolve] Q (*corr.*); Adsolve Q   30. weal] Q (*corr.*); veale Q
(*uncorr.*).   (*uncorr.*).
                                        37. Troy] *Dodsley*; Trope Q.

30. *proper weal*] personal well-being.

You shall hear odds betwixt your son and mine.

Marc Antonio retires himself.

VALERIO.

Tell him I cannot do't. Shall I be made   40
A foolish novice, my purse set abroach
By every cheating come-you-seven, to lend
My money and be laugh'd at? Tell him plain
I profess husbandry, and will not play
The prodigal like him gainst my profession.   45

GOSTANZO [*aside*].

Here's a son.

MARC ANTONIO [*aside*].   An admirable spark.

PAGE.

Well, sir, I'll tell him so.   *Exit* Page.

VALERIO.   'Sfoot, let him lead
A better husband's life and live not idly,
Spending his time, his coin, and self on wenches.

GOSTANZO.

Why, what's the matter, son?   50

VALERIO.

Cry mercy, sir. Why, there come messengers
From this and that brave gallant, and such gallants
As I protest I saw but through a grate.

GOSTANZO.

And what's this message?

VALERIO.   Faith, sir, he's disappointed
Of payments and disfurnish'd of means present.   55
If I would do him the kind office, therefore,
To trust him but some seven-night with the keeping
Of forty crowns for me, he deeply swears,
As he's a gentleman, to discharge his trust.
And that I shall eternally endear him   60
To my wish'd service, he protests and contests.

GOSTANZO.

Good words, Valerio. But thou art too wise

39.1.] *Parrott*; after *l. 37 in Q*.

---

39. *hear odds*] learn the difference.
42. *come-you-seven*] gambler.
53. *through a grate*] i.e., through a grated window, as perhaps of a prison.

To be deceiv'd by breath. I'll turn thee loose
To the most cunning cheater of them all.

VALERIO.

'Sfoot, he's not asham'd besides to charge me   65
With a late promise. I must yield, indeed,
I did (to shift him with some contentment)
Make such a frivol promise.

GOSTANZO.   Ay, well done.
Promises are no fetters. With that tongue
Thy promise pass'd, unpromise it again.   70
Wherefore has man a tongue of power to speak,
But to speak still to his own private purpose?
Beasts utter but one sound, but men have change
Of speech and reason, even by Nature given them,
Now to say one thing and another now,   75
As best may serve their profitable ends.

MARC ANTONIO [aside].

By'r-lady, sound instructions to a son.

VALERIO.

Nay, sir, he makes his claim by debt of friendship.

GOSTANZO.

Tush, friendship's but a term, boy. The fond world
Like to a doting mother glazes over   80
Her children's imperfections with fine terms.
What she calls friendship and true, humane kindness,
Is only want of true experience.
Honesty is but a defect of wit;
Respect but mere rusticity and clownery.   85

MARC ANTONIO [aside].

Better and better. Soft, here comes my son.

Enter Fortunio, Rinaldo, *and* Gratiana.

RINALDO [aside].

Fortunio, keep your countenance. —[*To* Gostanzo.]   See,
sir, here

---

67. *shift ... contentment*] get rid of him with something that would
satisfy him.

79. *fond*] foolish, with perhaps an overtone of the present meaning of the
word.

85. *clownery*] boorishness.

The poor young married couple which you pleas'd
To send for to your house.

GOSTANZO.   Fortunio, welcome.
And in that welcome I employ your wife's,   90
Who I am sure you count your second self.   *He kisses her.*

FORTUNIO.
Sir, your right noble favors do exceed
All power of worthy gratitude by words,
That in your care supply my father's place.

GOSTANZO.
Fortunio, I cannot choose but love you,   95
Being son to him who long time I have lov'd,
From whose just anger my house shall protect you,
Till I have made a calm way to your meetings.

FORTUNIO.
I little thought, sir, that my father's love
Would take so ill so slight a fault as this.   100

GOSTANZO.
Call you it slight? Nay, though his spirit take it
In higher manner than for your lov'd sake
I would have wish'd him, yet I make a doubt,
Had my son done the like, if my affection
Would not have turn'd to more spleen than your father's.   105
And yet I qualify him all I can,
And doubt not but that time and my persuasion
Will work out your excuse, since youth and love
Were th'unresisted organs to seduce you.
But you must give him leave, for fathers must   110
Be won by penitence and submission,
And not by force or opposition.

FORTUNIO.
Alas, sir, what advise you me to do?
I know my father to be highly mov'd,
And am not able to endure the breath   115

109. organs] *Dodsley*; organies *Q*.

---

103. *make a doubt*] suspect.
106. *qualify*] pacify.
109. *organs*] instruments.

Of his express'd displeasure, whose hot flames
I think my absence soonest would have quench'd.
GOSTANZO.
   True, sir, as fire with oil, or else like them
That quench the fire with pulling down the house.
You shall remain here in my house conceal'd   120
Till I have won your father to conceive
Kinder opinion of your oversight.
Valerio, entertain Fortunio
And his fair wife, and give them conduct in.
VALERIO.
   Y'are welcome, sir.
GOSTANZO.   What, sirrah, is that all?   125
No entertainment to the gentlewoman?
VALERIO.
   Forsooth, y'are welcome by my father's leave.
GOSTANZO.
   What, no more compliment? Kiss her, you sheepshead.
Why, when? —Go, go, sir, call your sister hither.
                            Exit Valerio.
Lady, you'll pardon our gross bringing up?   130
We dwell far off from court, you may perceive.
The sight of such a blazing star as you
Dazzles my rude son's wits.
GRATIANA.   Not so, good sir.
The better husband, the more courtly ever.
RINALDO.
   Indeed a courtier makes his lips go far,   135
As he doth all things else.

          Enter Valerio, Bellanora.

GOSTANZO.   Daughter, receive
This gentlewoman home, and use her kindly.
                            She kisses her.
BELLANORA.
   My father bids you kindly welcome, lady,
And therefore you must needs come well to me.

---

126. *entertainment*] courteous greeting; in this case, a kiss.

GRATIANA.

    Thank you, forsooth.

GOSTANZO.   Go, dame, conduct 'em in.   140

           Exeunt Rinaldo, Fortunio, Bellanora, Gratiana.

Ah, errant sheepshead, hast thou liv'd thus long,
And dar'st not look a woman in the face?
Though I desire especially to see
My son a husband, shall I therefore have him
Turn absolute cullion? Let's see, kiss thy hand.   145
Thou kiss thy hand? Thou wip'st thy mouth, by th' mass.
Fie on thee, clown. They say the world's grown finer,
But I for my part never saw young men
Worse fashion'd and brought up than nowadays.
'Sfoot, when myself was young, was not I kept   150
As far from court as you? I think I was.
And yet my father on a time invited
The Duchess of his house. I, being then
About some five-and-twenty years of age,
Was thought the only man to entertain her.   155
I had my congé—plant myself of one leg,
Draw back the tother with a deep-fetch'd honor,
Then with a bel-regard advant mine eye
With boldness on her very visnomy.
Your dancers all were counterfeits to me.   160
And for discourse in my fair mistress' presence
I did not as you barren gallants do,
Fill my discourses up drinking tobacco,
But on the present furnish'd evermore
With tales and practic'd speeches—as sometimes,   165
"What is't o'clock?" "What stuff's this petticoat?"
"What cost the making?" "What the fringe and all?"
And what she had under her petticoat,
And such-like witty compliments. And for need,

---

141. *errant*] absolute, unmitigated.
145. *cullion*] "A base, despicable, or vile fellow; a rascal" (*OED*).
153. *Duchess . . . house*] family matriarch, head of his house.
157. *honor*] curtsy or bow.
158. *bel-regard*] flirtatious glance.
158. *advant*] advance.
163. *drinking*] inhaling.

I could have written as good prose and verse   170
As the most beggarly poet of 'em all,
Either acrostic, exordium,
Epithalamions, satires, epigrams,
Sonnets in dozens, or your quatorzains
In any rhyme, masculine, feminine,   175
Or sdrucciola, or couplets, blank verse.
Y'are but bench-whistlers nowadays to them
That were in our times. Well, about your husbandry.
Go, for i'faith, th'art fit for nothing else.

                     Exit Valerio. *Prodit* Marc Antonio.

MARC ANTONIO.

By'r-lady, you have play'd the courtier rarely.   180

GOSTANZO.

But did you ever see so blank a fool,
When he should kiss a wench, as my son is?

MARC ANTONIO.

Alas, 'tis but a little bashfulness.
You let him keep no company, nor allow him
Money to spend at fence and dancing-schools.   185
Y'are too severe, i'faith.

GOSTANZO.   And you too supple.
Well, sir, for your sake I have stay'd your son
From flying to the wars. Now see you rate him,
To stay him yet from more expenseful courses,
Wherein your lenity will encourage him.   190

MARC ANTONIO.

Let me alone. I thank you for this kindness.   *Exeunt.*

            Enter Valerio *and* Rinaldo.

RINALDO.

So, are they gone? Now tell me, brave Valerio,
Have I not won the wreath from all your wits,

---

172. *exordium*] not a literary form as such, but simply the rhetorical term
for the beginning of something, particularly an oration or discourse.

174. *Sonnets in dozens*] "probably songs or sonnets of twelve lines in
length" (Parrott).

174. *quatorzains*] French term for sonnet.

176. *sdrucciola*] a rhyme word in which the third syllable from the end
of the word is accented, i.e., a dactylic rime. So called from the Italian
sdrucciolo (slippery).

177. *bench-whistlers*] do-nothings.   179.1. *Prodit*] comes forward.

Brought thee t'enjoy the most desired presence
Of thy dear love at home, and with one labor   195
My brother t'enjoy thy sister, where
It had been her undoing t'have him seen,
And make thy father crave what he abhors,
T'entreat my brother home t'enjoy his daughter,
Command thee kiss thy wench, chide for not kissing,   200
And work all this out of a Machiavel,
A miserable politician?
I think the like was never play'd before!

VALERIO.

Indeed, I must commend thy wit of force.
And yet I know not whose deserves most praise,   205
Of thine or my wit. Thine for plotting well,
Mine, that durst undertake and carry it
With such true form.

RINALDO.   Well, th'evening crowns the day.
Persever to the end. My wit hath put
Blind Fortune in a string into your hand.   210
Use it discreetly, keep it from your father,
Or you may bid all your good days good-night.

VALERIO.

Let me alone, boy.

RINALDO.   Well, sir, now to vary
The pleasures of our wits, thou know'st, Valerio,
Here is the new-turn'd gentleman's fair wife,   215
That keeps thy wife and sister company,
With whom the amorous courtier Dariotto
Is far in love, and of whom her sour husband
Is passing jealous, puts on eagle's eyes
To pry into her carriage. Shall we see   220
If he be now from home, and visit her?

Enter Gazetta *sewing,* Cornelio *following.*

See, see, the prisoner comes.

VALERIO.   But soft, sir, see
Her jealous jailor follows at her heels.
Come, we will watch some fitter time to board her,

---

204. *of force*] necessarily.
224. *board*] approach or accost.

And in the meantime seek out our mad crew.   225
My spirit longs to swagger.
RINALDO.   Go to, youth.
Walk not too boldly. If the sergeants meet you,
You may have swaggering work your bellyful.
VALERIO.
No better copesmates.

> Gazetta *sits and sings sewing.*

I'll go seek 'em out with this light in my hand.   230
The slaves grow proud with seeking out of us.
> *Exeunt* [Valerio *and* Rinaldo].
CORNELIO.
A pretty work. I pray what flowers are these?
GAZETTA.
The pansy this.
CORNELIO.   O, that's for lover's thoughts.
What's that, a columbine?
GAZETTA.   No, that thankless flower
Fits not my garden.
CORNELIO.   Hmnn! Yet it may mine.   235
This were a pretty present for some friend,
Some gallant courtier, as for Dariotto,
One that adores you in his soul, I know.
GAZETTA.
Me? Why me more than yourself, I pray?
CORNELIO.
O yes, he adores you, and adhorns me.   240
I'faith, deal plainly, do not his kisses relish
Much better than such peasant's as I am?
GAZETTA.
Whose kisses?

235. Hmnn!] *this edn.*; Him? *Q*;
Hem! *Dodsley.*

---

229. *copesmates*] either "adversaries" or "associates."
230. *this light*] "his sword" (Parrott).
233. *pansy*] French *pensée*, thought.
234. *columbine*] the cuckold's flower because of its horn-like spurs.
240. *adhorns*] to plant horns on, to cuckold, with the added implication
of "adorn."

CORNELIO.   Dariotto's. Does he not
   The thing you wot on?
GAZETTA.   What thing, good lord?
CORNELIO.
   Why, lady, lie with you!
GAZETTA.   Lie with me?   245
CORNELIO.
   Ay, with you.
GAZETTA.   You with me, indeed!
CORNELIO.
   Nay, I am told that he lies with you too,
   And that he is the only whoremaster
   About the city.
GAZETTA.   If he be so only,
   'Tis a good hearing that there are no more.   250
CORNELIO.
   Well, mistress, well. I will not be abus'd.
   Think not you dance in nets, for though you do not
   Make broad profession of your love to him,
   Yet do I understand your darkest language,
   Your treads o'th' toe, your secret jogs and wrings,   255
   Your intercourse of glances. Every tittle
   Of your close amorous rites I understand.
   They speak as loud to me as if you said,
   "My dearest Dariotto, I am thine."
GAZETTA.
   Jesus, what moods are these? Did ever husband   260
   Follow his wife with jealousy so unjust?
   That once I lov'd you, you yourself will swear.
   And if I did, where did you lose my love?
   Indeed, this strange and undeserved usage
   Hath power to shake a heart were ne'er so settled.   265
   But I protest all your unkindness never
   Had strength to make me wrong you but in thought.

---

244. *wot on*] think about.
246. *Ay*] consistently spelled *I* in the original quarto, thus visually supporting the homonym Gazetta picks up in the next line.
248. *only whoremaster*] best, most pre-eminent lecher.
252. *dance in nets*] pass unnoticed.
253. *broad profession*] profess your love for him openly.

CORNELIO.

No, not with Dariotto?

GAZETTA.   No, by heaven.

CORNELIO.

No letters pass'd, nor no designs for meeting?

GAZETTA.

No, by my hope of heaven.

CORNELIO.   Well, no time past.   270

Go, go; go in and sew.

GAZETTA.   Well, be it so.   *Exit* Gazetta.

CORNELIO.

Suspicion is (they say) the first degree
Of deepest wisdom. And however others
Inveigh against this mood of jealousy,
For my part I suppose it the best curb   275
To check the ranging appetites that reign
In this weak sex. My neighbors point at me
For this my jealousy. But should I do
As most of them do, let my wife fly out
To feasts and revels, and invite home gallants,   280
Play Menelaus, give them time and place,
While I sit like a well-taught waiting-woman,
Turning her eyes upon some work or picture,
Read in a book, or take a feigned nap,
While her kind lady takes one to her lap?   285
No, let me still be pointed at, and thought
A jealous ass, and not a wittolly knave.
I have a shew of courtiers haunt my house,
In show my friends, and for my profit too.
But I perceive 'em, and will mock their aims   290
With looking to their mark, I warrant 'em.

---

281. *Play Menelaus*] Menelaus hospitably entertained Paris, who came to
rob him of his wife.

285. *takes ... lap*] copulates; a common Renaissance euphemism.
Cf. Hamlet's remarks to Ophelia (III.ii.108–114).

287. *wittolly knave*] husband who permits his wife's adultery.

288. *shew*] show; a strange, bizzare display, a spectacle.

290. *perceive 'em*] see through them.

290–291. *mock ... mark*] make them misfire by keeping close watch on
their target (i.e., Gazetta).

I am content to ride abroad with them,
To revel, dice, and fit their other sports,
But by their leaves I'll have a vigilant eye
To the main chance still. See my brave comrades.   295

Enter Dariotto, Claudio, [*Page*] *and* Valerio, Valerio *putting up his sword.*

DARIOTTO [*to* Valerio].

Well, wag, well. Wilt thou still deceive thy father,
And being so simple a poor soul before him,
Turn swaggerer in all companies besides?

CLAUDIO.

Hadst thou been rested, all would have come forth.

VALERIO.

Soft, sir, there lies the point. I do not doubt   300
But t' have my pennyworths of these rascals one day.
I'll smoke the buzzing hornets from their nests,
Or else I'll make their leather jerkins stay.
The whoreson hungry horseflies. Foot, a man
Cannot so soon, for want of almanacs,   305
Forget his day but three or four bare months,
But straight he sees a sort of corporals
To lie in ambuscado to surprise him.

DARIOTTO.

Well, thou hadst happy fortune to escape 'em.

VALERIO.

But they thought theirs was happier to scape me.   310
I, walking in the place where men's lawsuits
Are heard and pleaded, not so much as dreaming
Of any such encounter, steps me forth
Their valiant foreman, with the word, "I rest you."

307. sees] *Parrott*; fees *Q*.

---

293. *fit*] satisfy the requirements of.
299. *rested*] arrested.
301. *pennyworths*] money's worth, i.e., revenge.
303. *leather jerkins*] "the buff-coats of the sergeants who arrested debtors" (Parrott).
306. *his day*] when payment for debt is due.
307. *corporals*] the underlings of the sergeants. Valerio is extending the military image implicit in the word *sergeant* here and in the word *ambuscado* in the next line.

I made no more ado, but laid these paws   315
Close on his shoulders, tumbling him to earth.
And there sate he on his posteriors,
Like a baboon. And turning me about,
I straight espied the whole troop issuing on me.
I stepp'd me back, and drawing my old friend here,   320
Made to the midst of them, and all unable
T'endure the shock, all rudely fell in rout,
And down the stairs they ran with such a fury,
As meeting with a troop of lawyers there,
Mann'd by their clients, some with ten, some with twenty, 325
Some five, some three—he that had least, had one—
Upon the stairs they bore them down afore them.
But such a rattling then was there amongst them
Of ravish'd declarations, replications,
Rejoinders and petitions—all their books   330
And writings torn and trod on, and some lost—
That the poor lawyers coming to the bar,
Could say nought to the matter, but instead,
Were fain to rail and talk besides their books
Without all order.
CLAUDIO.   Faith, that same vein of railing   335
Became now most applausive. Your best poet is
He that rails grossest.
DARIOTTO.   True, and your best fool
Is your broad railing fool.
VALERIO.   And why not, sir?
For by the gods, to tell the naked truth,
What objects see men in this world but such   340
As would yield matter to a railing humor,
When he that last year carried after one
An empty buckram bag now fills a coach,

---

315. *Mann'd*] defended by, as though they were a frigate or a fort.

329. *replications*] "The reply of the plaintiff to the plea or answer of the defendant, being the third step in common pleadings" (*OED*).

334. *fain*] forced by circumstances.

334. *besides their books*] extemporaneously.

338. *broad*] bawdy, indecent.

343. *buckram bag*] bag made of cheap, coarse cloth stiffened with gum or paste, also known as "a lawyer's bag."

And crowds the senate with such troops of clients
And servile followers, as would put a mad spleen   345
Into a pigeon?
DARIOTTO.   Come, pray leave these cross capers.
Let's make some better use of precious time.
See, here's Cornelio. Come, lad, shall we to dice?
CORNELIO.
Anything, I.
CLAUDIO.   Well said. How does thy wife?
CORNELIO.
In health, God save her.
VALERIO.   But where is she, man?   350
CORNELIO.
Abroad about her business.
VALERIO.   Why, not at home?
Foot, my masters, take her to the court,
And this rare lad, her husband. And—dost hear?—
Play me no more the miserable farmer,
But be advis'd by friends. Sell all i'th' country,   355
Be a flat courtier, follow some great man,
Or bring thy wife there, and she'll make thee great.
CORNELIO.
What, to the court? Then take me for a gull.
VALERIO.
Nay, never shun it to be call'd a gull,
For I see all the world is but a gull,   360
One man gull to another in all kinds.
A merchant to a courtier is a gull,
A client to a lawyer is a gull,
A married man to a bachelor, a gull,
A bachelor to a cuckold is a gull,   365
All to a poet, or a poet to himself.
CORNELIO [aside].
Hark, Dariotto, shall we gull this guller?
DARIOTTO [aside].
He gulls his father, man, we cannot gull him.
CORNELIO [aside].
Let me alone. —Of all men's wits alive
I most admire Valerio's, that hath stol'n   370

---

356. *flat*] outright.

By his mere industry, and that by spurts,
Such qualities as no wit else can match
With plodding at perfection every hour,
Which, if his father knew each gift he has,
Were like enough to make him give all from him. 375
I mean, besides his dicing and his wenching,
He has stol'n languages, th'Italian, Spanish,
And some spice of the French, besides his dancing,
Singing, playing on choice instruments.
These has he got, almost against the hair. 380

CLAUDIO.
But hast thou stol'n all these, Valerio?

VALERIO.
Toys, toys, a pox. And yet they be such toys
As every gentleman would not be without.

CORNELIO.
Vainglory makes ye judge 'em light i'faith!

DARIOTTO.
Afore heaven I was much deceiv'd in him. 385
But he's the man indeed that hides his gifts,
And sets them not to sale in every presence.
I would have sworn his soul were far from music,
And that all his choice music was to hear
His fat beasts bellow.

CORNELIO.　　　　　Sir, your ignorance 390
Shall eftsoon be confuted. Prithee, Val,
Take thy theorbo for my sake a little.

VALERIO.
By heaven, this month I touch'd not a theorbo.

CORNELIO.
Touch'd a theorbo! Mark the very word.
Sirrah, go fetch. *Exit* Page. 395

384. '*em*] *Parrott*; on *Q*.

---

380. *against the hair*] "Usually the phrase means 'against one's natural
bent or inclination'. Here it seems to mean 'in spite of a seeming impossi-
bility'" (Parrott).

391. *eftsoon*] at once.

392. *theorbo*] "A large kind of lute with a double neck and two sets of
tuning-pegs . . .; much in vogue in the 17th century" (*OED*).

394. *Touch'd*] "The proper technical word for playing upon the theorbo"
(Parrott).

VALERIO.

    If you will have it, I must needs confess

    I am no husband of my qualities.   *He untrusses and capers.*

CORNELIO.

    See what a caper there was!

CLAUDIO.   See again!

CORNELIO.

    The best that ever. And how it becomes him!

DARIOTTO.

    O that his father saw these qualities!   400

Enter a Page *with an instrument.*

CORNELIO.

    Nay, that's the very wonder of his wit,

    To carry all without his father's knowledge.

DARIOTTO.

    Why, we might tell him now.

CORNELIO.   No, but we could not,

    Although we think we could. His wit doth charm us.

    Come, sweet Val, touch and sing.

DARIOTTO [*aside*].   Foot, will you hear   405

    The worst voice in Italy?

Enter Rinaldo.

CORNELIO.   O God, sir!   *He sings.*

    Courtiers, how like you this?

DARIOTTO.   Believe it, excellent!

CORNELIO.

    Is it not natural?

VALERIO.   If my father heard me,

    Foot, he'd renounce me for his natural son.

DARIOTTO.

    By heaven, Valerio, and I were thy father,   410

---

    397. *I am . . . qualities*] i.e., "I do not hide my good points." Valerio is also using the usual pun on *husband* in the play.

    397. *S.D. untrusses and capers*] loosens his clothes and cuts a caper.

    408. *natural*] unforced, with probably a secondary meaning of "foolish" or "ridiculous."

    409. *natural*] legitimate.

    410. *and*] if.

And lov'd good qualities as I do my life,
I'd disinherit thee, for I never heard
Dog howl with worse grace.

CORNELIO.   Go to, Signor Courtier.
You deal not courtly now to be so plain,
Nor nobly, to discourage a young gentleman   415
In virtuous qualities, that has but stol'n 'em.

CLAUDIO.
Call you this touching a theorbo?

OMNES.   Ha, ha, ha!
Exeunt all but Valerio *and* Rinaldo.

VALERIO.
How now, what's here?

RINALDO.   Zoons, a plot laid to gull thee.
Could thy wit think the voice was worth the hearing?
This was the courtier's and the cuckold's project.   420

VALERIO.
And is't e'en so? 'Tis very well, Mast Courtier
And Dan Cornuto, I'll cry quit with both.
And first, I'll cast a jar betwixt them both,
With firing the poor cuckold's jealousy.
I have a tale will make him mad,   425
And turn his wife divorced loose amongst us.
But first let's home, and entertain my wife.
O father, pardon. I was born to gull thee.   *Exeunt.*

Finis Actus Secundi.

[III.i]
Enter Fortunio, Bellanora, Gratiana, Gostanzo *following closely.*

FORTUNIO.
How happy am I, that by this sweet means
I gain access to your most loved sight,
And therewithal to utter my full love,
Which but for vent would burn my entrails up!

---

421. *Mast*] shortened form of "Master."
422. *Cornuto*] cuckold.
422. *cry quit with*] get even with.
423. *cast a jar*] start a quarrel.

GOSTANZO [*aside*].

    By th' mass they talk too softly.

BELLANORA.   Little thinks   5

    The austere mind my thrifty father bears
    That I am vow'd to you, and so am bound
    From him who for more riches he would force
    On my disliking fancy.

FORTUNIO.   'Tis no fault

    With just deeds to defraud an injury.   10

GOSTANZO [*aside*].

    My daughter is persuading him to yield
    In dutiful submission to his father.

Enter Valerio.

VALERIO.

    Do I not dream? Do I behold this sight
    With waking eyes? Or from the ivory gate
    Hath Morpheus sent a vision to delude me?   15
    Is't possible that I, a mortal man,
    Should shrine within mine arms so bright a goddess,
    The fair Gratiana, beauty's little world?

GOSTANZO [*aside*].

    What have we here?

VALERIO.

    My dearest mine of gold,   20
    All this that thy white arms enfold,
    Account it as thine own freehold.

GOSTANZO [*aside*].

    God's my dear soul, what sudden change is here!
    I smell how this gear will fall out, i'faith.

VALERIO.

    Fortunio, sister, come. Let's to the garden.   *Exeunt.*   25

GOSTANZO.

    Sits the wind there, i'faith? See what example
    Will work upon the dullest appetite.

---

    14. *ivory gate*] the gate of false dreams, according to Homer (*Odyssey*, XIX, 562) and Vergil (*Aeneid*, VI, 893–896).

    22. *freehold*] estate held for as long as one lives.

    24. *gear*] business.

My son, last day so bashful that he durst not
Look on a wench, now courts her, and, by'r lady,
Will make his friend Fortunio wear his head   30
Of the right modern fashion. What, Rinaldo!

Enter Rinaldo.

RINALDO.
    I fear I interrupt your privacy.
GOSTANZO.
    Welcome, Rinaldo, would't had been your hap
    To come a little sooner, that you might
    Have seen a handsome sight. But let that pass.   35
    The short is that your sister Gratiana
    Shall stay no longer here.
RINALDO.   No longer, sir?
    Repent you then so soon your favor to her,
    And to my brother?
GOSTANZO.   No so, good Rinaldo.
    But to prevent a mischief that I see   40
    Hangs over your abused brother's head.
    In brief, my son has learn'd but too much courtship.
    It was my chance even now to cast mine eye
    Into a place where, to your sister, enter'd
    My metamorphos'd son—I must conceal   45
    What I saw there. But to be plain, I saw
    More than I would see. I had thought to make
    My house a kind receipt for your kind brother.
    But I'd be loath his wife should find more kindness
    Than she had cause to like of.
RINALDO.   What's the matter?   50
    Perhaps a little compliment or so.
GOSTANZO.
    Well, sir, such compliment perhaps may cost
    Married Fortunio the setting on.
    Nor can I keep my knowledge. He that lately
    Before my face I could not get to look   55

---

31. *right modern fashion*] i.e., with cuckold's horns.
48. *receipt*] place of refuge.
53. *the setting on*] i.e., of horns.

Upon your sister, by this light, now kiss'd her,
Embrac'd and courted with as good a grace,
As any courtier could. And I can tell you
(Not to disgrace her) I perceiv'd the dame
Was as far forward as himself, by th' mass.   60

RINALDO.

You should have school'd him for't.

GOSTANZO.   No, I'll not see't,
For shame once found, is lost. I'll have him think
That my opinion of him is the same
That it was ever. It will be a mean
To bridle this fresh humor bred in him.   65

RINALDO.

Let me then school him. Foot, I'll rattle him up.

GOSTANZO.

No, no, Rinaldo, th'only remedy
Is to remove the cause, carry the object
From his late tempted eyes.

RINALDO.   Alas, sir, whither?
You know my father is incens'd so much   70
He'll not receive her.

GOSTANZO.   Place her with some friend
But for a time, till I reclaim your father.
Meantime your brother shall remain with me.

RINALDO (to himself).

The care's the less then. He has still his longing
To be with this gull's daughter.

GOSTANZO.   What resolve you?   75
I am resolv'd she lodges here no more.
My friend's son shall not be abus'd by mine.

RINALDO.

Troth, sir, I'll tell you what a sudden toy
Comes in my head. What think you if I brought her
Home to my father's house?

---

61. *school'd*] chastised.

62. *shame . . . lost*] according to Tilley, a variant of the proverb "Past
shame past amendment." Like many proverbs Gostanzo's version is too
elliptical to be completely clear. It probably means that once a person's
shameful act is *found*, in the sense of "discovered," he loses his sense of
shame, which would otherwise serve as a check on him.

GOSTANZO.   Ay, marry, sir.   80
    Would he receive her?
RINALDO.   Nay, you hear not all.
    I mean with use of some device or other.
GOSTANZO.
    As how, Rinaldo?
RINALDO.   Marry, sir, to say
    She is your son's wife, married past your knowledge.
GOSTANZO.
    I doubt last day he saw her, and will know her   85
    To be Fortunio's wife.
RINALDO.   Nay, as for that,
    I will pretend she was even then your son's wife,
    But feign'd by me to be Fortunio's
    Only to try how he would take the matter.
GOSTANZO.
    'Fore heaven 'twere pretty.
RINALDO.   Would it not do well?   90
GOSTANZO.
    Exceeding well, in sadness.
RINALDO.   Nay, good sir,
    Tell me unfeignedly, do ye like't indeed?
GOSTANZO.
    The best that e'er I heard.
RINALDO.   And do you think
    He'll swallow down the gudgeon?
GOSTANZO.   O' my life.
    It were a gross gob would not down with him,   95
    An honest knight, but simple, not acquainted
    With the fine sleights and policies of the world,
    As I myself am.
RINALDO.   I'll go fetch her straight.
    And this jest thrive, 'twill make us princely sport.
    But you must keep our counsel, second all,   100
    Which to make likely, you must needs sometimes

---

84. *past*] without.
85. *doubt*] fear, suspect.
91. *in sadness*] in earnest, seriously.
94. *gudgeon*] bait.
99. *And*] if.

Give your son leave (as if you knew it not)
To steal and see her at my father's house.

GOSTANZO.

Ay, but see you then that you keep good guard
Over his forward, new-begun affections,   105
For, by the Lord, he'll teach your brother else
To sing the cuckoo's note. Spirit will break out,
Though never so suppress'd and pinioned.

RINALDO.

Especially your son's. What would he be,
If you should not restrain him by good counsel?   110

GOSTANZO.

I'll have an eye on him, I warrant thee.
I'll in and warn the gentlewoman to make ready.

RINALDO.

Well, sir, and I'll not be long after you.   *Exit* Gostanzo.
Heaven, heaven, I see these politicians
(Out of blind Fortune's hands) are our most fools. 115
'Tis she that gives the luster to their wits,
Still plodding at traditional devices.
But take 'em out of them to present actions,
A man may grope and tickle 'em like a trout,
And take 'em from their close dear holes as fat   120
As a physician, and as giddy-headed,
As if by miracle heaven had taken from them
Even that which commonly belongs to fools.
Well, now let's note what black ball of debate
Valerio's wit hath cast betwixt Cornelio   125
And the enamor'd courtier. I believe
His wife and he will part. His jealousy
Hath ever watch'd occasion of divorce,
And now Valerio's villainy will present it.
See, here comes the twin-courtier, his companion.   130

Enter Claudio.

122. by] *Dodsley*; be *Q*.

---

107. *To . . . note*] i.e., to be a cuckold.
115. *Out . . . hands*] i.e., when they are not helped by Fortune.
119. *tickle 'em*] a common method of catching trout by tickling them
about the gills.

CLAUDIO.

    Rinaldo, well encounter'd.

RINALDO.   Why? What news?

CLAUDIO.

    Most sudden and infortunate, Rinaldo.
    Cornelio is incens'd so 'gainst his wife
    That no man can procure her quiet with him.
    I have assay'd him, and made Marc Antonio   135
    With all his gentle rhetoric second me.
    Yet all, I fear me, will be cast away.
    See, see, they come. Join thy wit, good Rinaldo,
    And help to pacify his yellow fury.

RINALDO.

    With all my heart. I consecrate my wit   140
    To the wish'd comfort of distressed ladies.

      Enter Cornelio, Marc Antonio, Valerio, Page.

CORNELIO.

    Will any man assure me of her good behavior?

VALERIO.

    Who can assure a jealous spirit? You may be afraid of
    the shadow of your ears, and imagine them to be horns.
    If you will assure yourself, appoint keepers to watch 145
    her.

CORNELIO.

    And who shall watch the keepers?

MARC ANTONIO.

    To be sure of that, be you her keeper.

VALERIO.

    Well said, and share the horns yourself, for that's the
    keeper's fee.   150

CORNELIO.

    But say I am gone out of town, and must trust others.
    How shall I know if those I trust be trusty to me?

RINALDO.

    Marry, sir, by a singular instinct, given naturally to all

---

139. *yellow fury*] jealousy.

147. *And . . . keepers*] "Cf. Juvenal's phrase: *Quis custodiet ipsos custodes* (*Satire VI*, 347–8)" (Parrott). By Chapman's time it had become a common English proverb; see Tilley, K 13.

150. *keeper's fee*] The hide and horns were usually the gamekeeper's fee.

you married men, that if your wives play leger-de-heel,
though you be a hundred miles off, yet you shall be sure 155
instantly to find it in your foreheads.

CORNELIO.

Sound doctrine, I warrant you. I am resolved, i'faith.

PAGE.

Then give me leave to speak, sir, that hath all this while
been silent. I have heard you with extreme patience.
Now, therefore, prick up your ears, and vouchsafe me 160
audience.

CLAUDIO.

Good boy, o' mine honor.

CORNELIO.

Pray, what are you, sir?

PAGE.

I am here, for default of better, of counsel with the fair
Gazetta. And though herself had been best able to defend 165
herself if she had been here, and would have pleased to
put forth the buckler which Nature hath given all women—
I mean her tongue—

VALERIO.

Excellent good boy.

PAGE.

Yet since she either vouchsafes it not, or thinks her innocence 170
a sufficient shield against your jealous accusations, I
will presume to undertake the defense of that absent and
honorable lady, whose sworn knight I am, and in her of all
that name (for lady is grown a common name to their whole
sex), which sex I have ever loved from my youth, and shall 175
never cease to love, till I want wit to admire.

MARC ANTONIO.

An excellent spoken boy.

VALERIO.

Give ear, Cornelio. Here is a young Mercurio sent to
persuade thee.

---

154. *leger-de-heel*] literally "light-heeled," a cant phrase for female
wantonness.
178. *Mercurio*] Mercury, the god of eloquence (and craftiness and
thievery).

CORNELIO.

Well, sir, let him say on.   180

PAGE.

It is a heavy case to see how this light sex is tumbled
and tossed from post to pillar under the unsavory breath
of every humorous peasant. Gazetta, you said, is unchaste,
disloyal, and I wot not what. Alas, is it her fault? Is
she not a woman? Did she not suck it (as others of her   185
sex do) from her mother's breast? And will you condemn
that as her fault which is her nature? Alas, sir, you must
consider a woman is an unfinished creature, delivered hastily
to the world before Nature had set to that seal which should
have made them perfect. Faults they have (no doubt) but   190
are we free? Turn your eye into yourself, good Signor
Cornelio, and weigh your own imperfections with hers. If she
be wanton abroad, are not you wanting at home? If she be
amorous, are not you jealous? If she be high set, are
not you taken down? If she be a courtesan, are not you a   195
cuckold?

CORNELIO.

Out, you rogue.

RINALDO.

On with thy speech, boy.

MARC ANTONIO.

You do not well, Cornelio, to discourage the bashful
youth.   200

CLAUDIO.

Forth, boy, I warrant thee.

PAGE.

But if our own imperfections will not teach us to bear
with theirs, yet let their virtues persuade us. Let us endure
their bad qualities for their good, allow the prickle for
the rose, the brack for the velvet, the paring for the cheese,   205
and so forth. If you say they range abroad, consider it is
nothing but to avoid idleness at home. Their nature is still

---

189. that seal] *membrum virile*.

204–205. *prickle . . . velvet*] "Parody of a well-known passage in Euphues:
'As therefore the sweetest rose hath his prickle, the finest velvet his brack, the
fairest flour his bran' (Lyly, *Works*, edited by Bond, vol. i, p. 184)" (Parrott).
A *brack* is a flaw in cloth.

to be doing; keep 'em a-doing at home. Let them practice
one good quality or other, either sewing, singing, playing,
chiding, dancing, or so, and these will put such idle toys 210
out of their heads into yours. But if you cannot find them
variety of business within doors, yet at least imitate the
ancient, wise citizens of this city, who used carefully to
provide their wives gardens near the town to plant, to graft
in, as occasion served, only to keep 'em from idleness.   215

VALERIO.

Everlasting good boy.

CORNELIO.

I perceive your knavery, sir, and will yet have
patience.

RINALDO.

Forth, my brave Curio.

PAGE.

As to her unquietness (which some have rudely termed 220
shrewishness), though the fault be in her, yet the cause
is in you. What so calm as the sea of its own nature? Art
was never able to equal it. Your dicing-tables, nor your
bowling alleys, are not comparable to it. Yet if a blast of
wind do but cross it, not so turbulent and violent an element 225
in the world. So (Nature in lieu of women's scarcity of wit,
having indued them with a large portion of will) if they may
(without impeach) enjoy their wills, no quieter creatures
under heaven. But if the breath of their husbands' mouths
once cross their wills, nothing more tempestuous. Why then, 230
sir, should you husbands cross your wives' wills thus,
considering the law allows them no wills at all at their

222. its] *Parrott*; it *Q*.

211–215. *But . . . idleness.*] The Page implies that the gardens will be
used as trysting places, like the *hortus conclusus* in Chaucer's *Merchant's Tale*.
Parrott, following Collier, quotes Stubbes' *Anatomy of Abuses* (1595):
"Then to these gardens they repair, when they [citizens' wives] list with a
basket and a boy, where they meeting their sweethearts, receive their
wished desires."

228. *impeach*] hindrance.

232. *no wills at all*] "By the Acts of 32 Henry VII, c. 1 and 34, 35 Henry
VIII, c. 5 married women were rendered incapable of devising real estate.
By common law in England a married woman could not . . . make a will
without her husband's consent until the *Married Women's Property Act* of
1882" (Parrott).

deaths, because it intended they should have their wills while they lived?

VALERIO.

Answer him but that, Cornelio.   235

CORNELIO.

All shall not serve her turn. I am thinking of other matters.

MARC ANTONIO.

Thou hast half won him, wag. Ply him yet a little further.

PAGE.

Now, sir, for these cuckooish songs of yours, of cuckolds, 240 horns, grafting, and such-like, what are they but mere imaginary toys, bred out of your own heads as your own, and so by tradition delivered from man to man, like scarecrows to terrify fools from this earthly paradise of wedlock, coined at first by some spent poets, superannated 245 bachelors, or some that were scarce men of their hands, who, like the fox, having lost his tail, would persuade others to lose theirs for company? Again, for your cuckold, what is it but a mere fiction? Show me any such creature in nature. If there be, I could never see it; neither could I ever find 250 any sensible difference betwixt a cuckold and a Christen creature. To conclude, let poets coin, or fools credit what they list. For mine own part, I am clear of this opinion, that your cuckold is a mere chimera, and that there are no cuckolds in the world—but those that have wives. And so I 255 will leave them.

CORNELIO.

'Tis excellent good, sir. I do take you, sir—d'ye see?—to be as it were bastard to the saucy courtier that would have me father more of your fraternity—d'ye see?—and so are instructed (as we hear) to second that villain with your 260 tongue, which he has acted with his tenure piece—d'ye see?

PAGE.

No such matter, o' my credit, sir.

---

245. *superannated*] superannuated.
246. *men . . . hands*] "men of prowess" (Parrott).
247. *like the fox*] Cf. I.i.92.

CORNELIO.

Well, sir, be as be may, I scorn to set my head against
yours—d'ye see?—when in the meantime I will firk your
father, whether you see or no.   *Exit drawing his rapier.* 265

RINALDO.

God's my life, Cornelio!   *Exit.*

VALERIO.

Have at your father, i'faith, boy, if he can find him.

MARC ANTONIO.

See, he comes here. He has missed him.

Enter Dariotto.

DARIOTTO.

How now, my hearts. What, not a wench amongst you?
'Tis a sign y'are not in the grace of wenches   270
That they will let you be thus long alone.

VALERIO.

Well, Dariotto, glory not too much
That for thy brisk attire and lips perfum'd,
Thou playest the stallion ever where thou com'st,
And like the husband of the flock, runn'st through   275
The whole town herd, and no man's bed secure,
No woman's honor unattempted by thee.
Think not to be thus fortunate forever,
But in thy amorous conquests at the last
Some wound will slice your mazer. Mars himself   280
Fell into Vulcan's snare, and so may you.

DARIOTTO.

Alas, alas. Faith, I have but the name.
I love to court and win, and the consent,
Without the act obtain'd, is all I seek.
I love the victory that draws no blood.   285

CLAUDIO.

O, 'tis a high desert in any man

---

264. *firk*] beat up, whip.
267.] The subject of the sentence is *He'll* understood.
280. *mazer*] head.
281. *Vulcan's snare*] the net Vulcan used to catch Venus and Mars
together in bed.

To be a secret lecher. I know some
That (like thyself) are true in nothing else.
MARC ANTONIO.
And, methinks, it is nothing if not told.
At least the joy is never full before. 290
VALERIO.
Well, Dariotto, th' hadst as good confess.
The sun shines broad upon your practices.
Vulcan will wake and intercept you one day.
DARIOTTO.
Why, the more jealous knave and coxcomb he.
What, shall the shaking of his bed a little 295
Put him in motion? It becomes him not.
Let him be dull'd and stal'd, and then be quiet.
The way to draw my custom to his house
Is to be mad and jealous. 'Tis the sauce
That whets my appetite.
VALERIO.   Or any man's. 300
Sine periculo friget lusus.
They that are jealous, use it still of purpose
To draw you to their houses.
DARIOTTO.   Ay, by heaven,
I am of that opinion. Who would steal
Out of a common orchard? Let me gain 305
My love with labor, and enjoy't with fear,
Or I am gone.

Enter Rinaldo.

RINALDO.   What, Dariotto here?
Foot, dar'st thou come near Cornelio's house?
DARIOTTO.
Why? Is the bull run mad? What ails he, trow?
RINALDO.
I know not what he ails, but I would wish you 310
To keep out of the reach of his sharp horns,
For by this hand he'll gore you.

---

301. *Sine . . . lusus*] "No fun without danger."
309. *trow*] do you suppose.

DARIOTTO.   And why me
     More than thyself, or these two other whelps?
     You all have basted him as well as I.
     I wonder what's the cause.
RINALDO.   Nay, that he knows,   315
     And swears withal that wheresoe'er he meets you,
     He'll mark you for a marker of men's wives.
VALERIO.
     Pray heaven he be not jealous by some tales
     That have been told him lately. Did you never
     Attempt his wife? Hath no love's harbinger,   320
     No looks, no letters, pass'd 'twixt you and her?
DARIOTTO.
     For looks I cannot answer. I bestow them
     At large and carelessly, much like the sun.
     If any be so foolish to apply them
     To any private fancy of their own   325
     (As many do), it's not my fault, thou knowest.
VALERIO.
     Well, Dariotto, this set face of thine
     (If thou be guilty of offense to him)
     Comes out of very want of wit and feeling
     What danger haunts thee. For Cornelio   330
     Is a tall man, I tell you, and 'twere best
     You shunn'd his sight awhile, till we might get
     His patience, or his pardon. For past doubt
     Thou diest if he but see thee.

                    Enter Cornelio.

RINALDO.   Foot, he comes.
DARIOTTO.
     Is this the cockatrice that kills with sight?   335
     How dost thou, boy? Ha?
CORNELIO.   Well.

322. looks] *Shepherd*; looke *Q*.

---

     314. *basted*] cuckolded.
     327. *set face*] unbending attitude.
     331. *tall man*] brave, good with a sword.
     335. *cockatrice*] a fabulous serpent who killed with a glance. Identified
with the Basilisk.

DARIOTTO.   What, lingering still
About this paltry town? Hadst thou been rul'd
By my advice, thou hadst by this time been
A gallant courtier, and at least a knight.
I would have got thee dubb'd by this time, certain.   340
CORNELIO.
And why then did you not yourself that honor?
DARIOTTO.
Tush, 'tis more honor still to make a knight
Than 'tis to be a knight, to make a cuckold
Than 'tis to be a cuckold.
CORNELIO.   Y'are a villain.
DARIOTTO.
God shield, man! Villain?
CORNELIO.   Ay, I'll prove thee one.   345
DARIOTTO.
What, wilt thou prove a villain?
By this light thou deceiv'st me, then.
CORNELIO.
Well, sir, thus I prove it.   *Draws.*
OMNES.   Hold, hold. Raise the streets.

[Cornelio *runs at him.*]

CLAUDIO.
Cornelio!
RINALDO.   Hold, Dariotto, hold!
VALERIO.   What, are thou hurt?
DARIOTTO.
A scratch, a scratch.
VALERIO.   Go, sirrah, fetch a surgeon.   350
                                             [*Exit* Page.]
CORNELIO.
You'll set a badge on the jealous fool's head, sir. Now
set a coxcomb on your own.
VALERIO.
What's the cause of these wars, Dariotto?
DARIOTTO.
Foot, I know not.
CORNELIO.
Well, sir, know and spare not. I will presently be divorced, 355
and then take her amongst ye.

RINALDO.

Divorc'd? Nay, good Cornelio.

CORNELIO.

By this sword, I will. The world shall not dissuade
me. *Exit.*

VALERIO.

Why this has been your fault now, Dariotto.   360
You youths have fashions, when you have obtain'd
A lady's favor, straight your hat must wear it,
Like a jackdaw that when he lights upon
A dainty morsel caws and makes his brags,
And then some kite doth scoop it from him straight,   365
Where if he fed without his dawish noise,
He might fare better, and have less disturbance.
Forbear it in this case, and when you prove
Victorious over fair Gazetta's fort,
Do not for pity sound your trump for joy,   370
But keep your valor close, and 'tis your honor.

Enter Page *and* Pock.

POCK.

God save you, Signor Dariotto.

DARIOTTO.

I know you not, sir. Your name, I pray?

POCK.

My name is Pock, sir, a practitioner in surgery.

DARIOTTO.

Pock, the surgeon. Y'are welcome, sir. I know a doctor 375
of your name, Master Pock.

POCK.

My name has made many doctors, sir.

RINALDO.

Indeed, 'tis a worshipful name.

VALERIO.

Marry is it, and of an ancient descent.

POCK.

Faith, sir, I could fetch my pedigree far, if I were so 380
disposed.

---

377. *My ... doctors*] referring to the pun in Pock's name. See list of
Actors.

RINALDO.

Out of France, at least.

POCK.

And if I stood on my arms, as others do—

DARIOTTO.

No, do not, Pock. Let other stand o' their arms, and thou
o' thy legs as long as thou canst.   385

POCK.

Though I live by my bare practice, yet I could show good
cards for my gentility.

VALERIO.

Tush, thou canst not shake off thy gentry, Pock. 'Tis bred
i'th' bone. But to the main, Pock. What thinkest thou of
this gentleman's wound, Pock? Canst thou cure it, Pock?   390

POCK.

The incision is not deep, nor the orifice exorbitant. The
pericranion is not dislocated. I warrant his life for forty
crowns, without perishing of any joint.

DARIOTTO.

Faith, Pock, 'tis a joint I would be loath to lose for the
best joint of mutton in Italy.   395

RINALDO.

Would such a scatch as this hazard a man's head?

POCK.

Ay, by'r-lady, sir. I have known some have lost their heads
for a less matter, I can tell you. Therefore, sir, you must
keep good diet. If you please to come home to my house
till you be perfectly cured, I shall have the more care 400
on you.

VALERIO.

That's your only course to have it well quickly.

POCK.

By what time would he have it well, sir?

396. hazard] *Collier*; hazards *Q*.

---

382. *Out of France*] To the English, syphilis was known as the French
disease; to the French, the Italian; to the Italians, the Spanish, etc.

383. *stood . . . arms*] made much of my ancestry, my coat of arms.

387. *cards*] proof. Probably genealogical tables.

388–389. *bred i'th' bone*] with a secondary reference to venereal disease.

391. *exorbitant*] too big.

395. *mutton*] prostitute.

DARIOTTO.

A very necessary question. Canst thou limit the time?

POCK.

O, sir, cures are like causes in law, which may be lengthened 405
or shortened at the discretion of the lawyer. He can either
keep it green with replications or rejoinders, or sometimes
skin it fair o'th' outside for fashion sake, but so he may be
sure 'twill break out again by a writ of error. And then
has he his suit new to begin. But I will convenant with 410
you, that by such a time I'll make your head as sound as
a bell, I will bring it to suppuration, and after I will make
it coagulate and grow to a perfect cicatrice. And all within
these ten days, so you keep a good diet.

DARIOTTO.

Well, come, Pock. We'll talk farther on't within. It draws 415
near dinner time. What's o'clock, boy?

PAGE.

By your clock, sir, it should be almost one, for your head
rung noon some half hour ago.

DARIOTTO.

Is't true, sir?

VALERIO.

Away, let him alone. Though he came in at the window, he 420
sets the gates of your honor open, I can tell you.

DARIOTTO.

Come in, Pock. Come, apply, and for this deed I'll give
the knave a wound shall never bleed. So, sir, I think this
knock rings loud acquittance for my ridiculous—

Exeunt all but Rinaldo *and* Valerio.

---

407. *replications or rejoinders*] replies. In law a *replication* is the reply of the
plaintiff to the defendant's plea; a *rejoinder* is the defendant's answer to the
plaintiff's replication.

409. *writ of error*] a writ calling for a new trial on the basis of error.

413. *cicatrice*] scar.

417–418. *head rung noon*] allusion to the proverb "To ring one's head at
noon," meaning to beat someone about the head. See Tilley, N 210.

420. *came . . . window*] a further reference to the Page as a bastard.
Cf. III.i.257–261, 267 above.

423. *a wound . . . bleed*] probably by cuckolding him.

424. *rings loud acquittance*] makes full payment.

Second my sad son's feign'd submission,
And see in all points how my brain will answer
His disguis'd grief with a set countenance
Of rage and choler. Now observe and learn
To school your son by me.

Intrant Rinaldo, Valerio, Gratiana.

MARC ANTONIO.   On with your mask.   75
Here come the other maskers, sir.
RINALDO.   Come on, I say.
Your father with submission will be calm'd.
Come on. Down o' your knees.   [Valerio *kneels*.]
GOSTANZO.   Villain, durst thou
Presume to gull thy father? Dost thou not
Tremble to see my bent and cloudy brows   80
Ready to thunder on thy graceless head,
And with the bolt of my displeasure cut
The thread of all my living from thy life,
For taking thus a beggar to thy wife?
VALERIO.   85
Father, if that part I have in your blood,
If tears, which so abundantly distil
Out of my inward eyes, and for a need
Can drown these outward—[*Aside to* Rinaldo.]   Lend me
     thy handkercher—
And being indeed as many drops of blood
Issuing from the creator of my heart,   90
Be able to beget so much compassion
Not on my life, but on this lovely dame,
Whom I hold dearer—
GOSTANZO.   Out upon thee, villain.
MARC ANTONIO.
Nay, good Gostanzo. Think you are a father.
GOSTANZO.
I will not hear a word. Out, out upon thee.   95
Wed without my advice, my love, my knowledge,
Ay, and a beggar too, a trull, a blowse!

---

75. *S.D. Intrant*] Enter.
97. *a trull, a blowse*] A *trull* is a whore. A *blowse* is a beggar's trull.

RINALDO.
Well, sir, to turn our heads to salve your license.   425
Since you have us'd the matter so unwisely
That now your father has discern'd your humor
In your too careless usage in his house,
Your wife must come from his house to Antonio's.
And he, to entertain her, must be told   430
She is not wife to his son, but to you,
Which news will make his simple wit triumph
Over your father. And your father, thinking
He still is gull'd, will still account him simple.
Come, sir, prepare your villainous wit to feign   435
A kind submission to your father's fury,
And we shall see what hearty policy
He will discover, in his feigned anger,
To blind Antonio's eyes, and make him think
He thinks her heartily to be your wife.   440
VALERIO.
O, I will gull him rarely with my wench
Low kneeling at my heels before his fury,
And injury shall be salv'd with injury.

Finis Actus Tertii.

[IV.i]   [*Enter*] Marc Antonio, Gostanzo.

MARC ANTONIO.
You see how too much wisdom evermore
Outshoots the truth. You were so forwards still
To tax my ignorance, my green experience
In these gray hairs, for giving such advantage
To my son's spirit that he durst undertake   5
A secret match so far short of his worth;
Your son so seasoned with obedience,
Even from his youth, that all his actions relish
Nothing but duty and your anger's fear.
What shall I say to you, if it fall out   10

---

425. *salve your license*] smooth over the liberties you took with Gratiana.
436. *kind*] natural.
437. *hearty policy*] "thorough-going dissimulation" (Parrott).

That this most precious son of yours has play'd
A part as bad as this, and as rebellious:
Nay, more, has grossly gull'd your wit withal?
What if my son has undergone the blame
That appertain'd to yours, and that this wench   15
With which my son is charg'd, may call you father?
Shall I then say you want experience?
Y'are green, y'are credulous; easy to be blinded.

GOSTANZO.

Ha, ha, ha.
Good Marc Antonio, when't comes to that,   20
Laugh at me, call me fool, proclaim me so.
Let all the world take knowledge I am an ass.

MARC ANTONIO.

O, the good God of Gods,
How blind is pride! What eagles we are still
In matters that belong to other men,   25
What beetles in our own! I tell you, knight,
It is confess'd to be as I have told you,
And Gratiana is by young Rinaldo
And your white son brought to me as his wife.
How think you now, sir?

GOSTANZO.   Even just as before,   30
And have more cause to think honest credulity
Is a true lodestone to draw on decrepity.
You have a heart too open to embrace
All that your ear receives. Alas, good man,
All this is but a plot for entertainment   35
Within your house, for your poor son's young wife
My house, without huge danger, cannot hold.

MARC ANTONIO.

Is't possible? What danger, sir, I pray?

GOSTANZO.

I'll tell you, sir. 'Twas time to take her thence.
My son that last day you saw could not frame   40

---

29. *white son*] fair-haired boy.
31–32.] "I have even more cause now to believe that credulity is a
magnet that attracts decrepitude to it"; i.e., "You are not only credulous,
you are becoming senile too."

His looks to entertain her, now by'r-lady,
Is grown a courtier. For myself, unseen,
Saw when he courted her, embrac'd and kiss'd h[e]
And I can tell you left not much undone
That was the proper office of your son.

MARC ANTONIO.

What world is this?

GOSTANZO.   I told this to Rinaldo,
Advising him to fetch her from my house,
And his young wit not knowing where to lodge h[er]
Unless with you, and saw that could not be
Without some wile, I presently suggested
This quaint device, to say she was my son's.
And all this plot, good Marc Antonio,
Flow'd from this fount only to blind your eyes.

MARC ANTONIO.

Out of how sweet a dream have you awak'd me
By heaven, I durst have laid my part in heaven
All had been true; it was so lively handled,
And drawn with such a seeming face of truth.
Your son had cast a perfect veil of grief
Over his face, for his so rash offense
To seal his love with act of marriage
Before his father had subscrib'd his choice.
My son (my circumstance lessening the fact)
Entreating me to break the matter to you,
And, joining my effectual persuasions
With your son's penitent submission,
Appease your fury, I at first assented,
And now expect their coming to that purpose.

GOSTANZO.

'Twas well. 'Twas well. Seem to believe it still.
Let art end what credulity began.
When they come, suit your words and looks to [

---

53. your] *Collier*; our *Q*.

62. *my circumstance ... fact*] "the circumstance tha[t]
shortly before had believed himself similarly slighted b[y]
had not been angry, serves to lessen in his eyes *the fact*, i.e. [
deceiving his father" (Parrott).
67. *expect*] await.

RINALDO [*aside to* Gostanzo].

    You thought not so last day, when you offer'd her

    A twelvemonths' board for one night's lodging with her.

GOSTANZO [*aside*].

    Go to, no more of that. Peace, good Rinaldo.   100

    It is a fault that only she and you know.

RINALDO [*aside*].

    Well, sir, go on, I pray.

GOSTANZO.   Have I, fond wretch,

    With utmost care and labor brought thee up,

    Ever instructing thee, omitting never

    The office of a kind and careful father,   105

    To make thee wise and virtuoûs like thy father,

    And hast thou in one act everted all,

    Proclaim'd thyself to all the world a fool,

    To wed a beggar?

VALERIO.   Father, say not so.

GOSTANZO.

    Nay, she's thy own. Here, rise, fool. Take her to thee;   110

    Live with her still. I know thou count'st thyself

    Happy in soul only in winning her.

    Be happy still. Here, take her hand, enjoy her.

    Would not a son hazard his father's wrath,

    His reputation in the world, his birthright,   115

    To have but such a mess of broth as this?

MARC ANTONIO.

    Be not so violent, I pray you, good Gostanzo.

    Take truce with passion; license your sad son

    To speak in his excuse.

GOSTANZO.   What! What excuse?

    Can any orator in this case excuse him?   120

    What can he say? What can be said of any?

VALERIO.

    Alas, sir, hear me. All that I can say

110. S.P. GOSTANZO] *Q* (*corr.*); *not
in Q* (*uncorr.*).

---

    107. *everted all*] turned everything upside down.

    115–116. *birthright . . . broth*] an allusion to Genesis 25:29–34, where
Esau sold his birthright for a mess of pottage.

    121. *What can be . . . any*] what can anyone say.

In my excuse is but to show love's warrant.
GOSTANZO [aside].
    Notable wag.
VALERIO.   I know I have committed
    A great impiety not to move you first   125
    Before the dame I meant to make my wife.
    Consider what I am, yet young and green.
    Behold what she is. Is there not in her,
    Ay, in her very eye, a power to conquer
    Even age itself and wisdom? Call to mind,   130
    Sweet father, what yourself being young have been.
    Think what you may be, for I do not think
    The world so far spent with you but you may
    Look back on such a beauty, and I hope
    To see you young again, and to live long   135
    With young affections. Wisdom makes a man
    Live young for ever, and where is this wisdom
    If not in you? Alas, I know not what
    Rests in your wisdom to subdue affections,
    But I protest it wrought with me so strongly   140
    That I had quite been drown'd in seas of tears,
    Had I not taken hold in happy time
    Of this sweet hand. My heart had been consum'd
    T'a heap of ashes with the flames of love,
    Had it not sweetly been assuag'd and cool'd   145
    With the moist kisses of these sugar'd lips.
GOSTANZO [aside].
    O, puissant wag. What huge large thongs he cuts
    Out of his friend Fortunio's stretching leather.
MARC ANTONIO [aside].
    He knows he does it but to blind my eyes.
GOSTANZO [aside].
    O, excellent! These men will put up anything.   150
VALERIO.
    Had I not had her, I had lost my life,
    Which life indeed I would have lost before

---

125. move] appeal to.
147–148.] "To cut large thongs of other men's leather" was a common
proverb. See Tilley, T 229.

I had displeas'd you, had I not receiv'd it
From such a kind, a wise, and honor'd father.
GOSTANZO [*aside*].

Notable boy!
VALERIO.   Yet do I here renounce   155
Love, life, and all, rather than one hour longer
Endure to have your love eclipsed from me.
GRATIANA.

O, I can hold no longer. If thy words
Be us'd in earnest, my Valerio,
Thou wound'st my heart, but I know 'tis in jest.   160
GOSTANZO [*aside*].

No, I'll be sworn she has her lyripoop too.
GRATIANA.

Didst thou not swear to love me spite of father
And all the world, that nought should sever us
But death itself?
VALERIO.   I did, but if my father
Will have his son forsworn, upon his soul   165
The blood of my black perjury shall lie,
For I will seek his favor though I die.
GOSTANZO.

No, no. Live still my son. Thou well shalt know,
I have a father's heart. Come, join your hands.
Still keep thy vows, and live together still,   170
Till cruel death set foot betwixt you both.
VALERIO.

O speak you this in earnest?
GOSTANZO.   Ay, by heaven.
VALERIO.

And never to recall it?
GOSTANZO.   Not till death.
RINALDO.

Excellent sir, you have done like yourself.
What would you more, Valerio?
VALERIO.   Worshipful father!   175

---

161. *she . . . lyripoop*] "has her wits about her. The word *lyripoop*, i.e. a
scarf or hood (lyripipium) worn by one who had taken a university degree,
was used figuratively to denote first learning, then wit or common sense"
(Parrott).

RINALDO.

    Come, sir, come you in, and celebrate your joys.

Exeunt all save the old men.

GOSTANZO.

    O Marc Antonio,

    Had I not arm'd you with an expectation,

    Would not this make you pawn your very soul

    The wench had been my son's wife?

MARC ANTONIO.   Yes, by heaven.   180

    A knavery thus effected might deceive

    A wiser man than I, for I, alas,

    Am no good politician. Plain believing,

    Simple honesty, is my policy still.

GOSTANZO.

    The visible marks of folly, honesty   185

    And quick credulity, his younger brother.

    I tell you, Marc Antonio, there is much

    In that young boy, my son.

MARC ANTONIO.   Not much honesty,

    If I may speak without offense to his father.

GOSTANZO.

    O God, you cannot please me better, sir.   190

    H'as honesty enough to serve his turn;

    The less honesty ever the more wit.

    But go you home, and use your daughter kindly.

    Meantime I'll school your son, and do you still

    Dissemble what you know. Keep off your son.   195

    The wench at home must still be my son's wife.

    Remember that, and be you blinded still.

MARC ANTONIO.

    You must remember, too, to let your son

    Use his accustom'd visitations,

    Only to blind my eyes.

GOSTANZO.   He shall not fail.   200

    But still take you heed, have a vigilant eye

    On that sly child of mine, for by this light,

    He'll be too bold with your son's forehead else.

MARC ANTONIO.

    Well, sir, let me alone. I'll bear a brain.   *Exeunt.*

---

204. *I'll ... brain*] a proverb meaning *I'll watch out*. See Tilley, B 596.

That this most precious son of yours has play'd
A part as bad as this, and as rebellious:
Nay, more, has grossly gull'd your wit withal?
What if my son has undergone the blame
That appertain'd to yours, and that this wench   15
With which my son is charg'd, may call you father?
Shall I then say you want experience?
Y'are green, y'are credulous; easy to be blinded.

GOSTANZO.

Ha, ha, ha.
Good Marc Antonio, when't comes to that,   20
Laugh at me, call me fool, proclaim me so.
Let all the world take knowledge I am an ass.

MARC ANTONIO.

O, the good God of Gods,
How blind is pride! What eagles we are still
In matters that belong to other men,   25
What beetles in our own! I tell you, knight,
It is confess'd to be as I have told you,
And Gratiana is by young Rinaldo
And your white son brought to me as his wife.
How think you now, sir?

GOSTANZO.   Even just as before,   30
And have more cause to think honest credulity
Is a true lodestone to draw on decrepity.
You have a heart too open to embrace
All that your ear receives. Alas, good man,
All this is but a plot for entertainment   35
Within your house, for your poor son's young wife
My house, without huge danger, cannot hold.

MARC ANTONIO.

Is't possible? What danger, sir, I pray?

GOSTANZO.

I'll tell you, sir. 'Twas time to take her thence.
My son that last day you saw could not frame   40

---

29. *white son*] fair-haired boy.
31–32.] "I have even more cause now to believe that credulity is a
magnet that attracts decrepitude to it"; i.e., "You are not only credulous,
you are becoming senile too."

RINALDO.

    Well, sir, to turn our heads to salve your license.   425
    Since you have us'd the matter so unwisely
    That now your father has discern'd your humor
    In your too careless usage in his house,
    Your wife must come from his house to Antonio's.
    And he, to entertain her, must be told   430
    She is not wife to his son, but to you,
    Which news will make his simple wit triumph
    Over your father. And your father, thinking
    He still is gull'd, will still account him simple.
    Come, sir, prepare your villainous wit to feign   435
    A kind submission to your father's fury,
    And we shall see what hearty policy
    He will discover, in his feigned anger,
    To blind Antonio's eyes, and make him think
    He thinks her heartily to be your wife.   440

VALERIO.

    O, I will gull him rarely with my wench
    Low kneeling at my heels before his fury,
    And injury shall be salv'd with injury.

Finis Actus Tertii.

[IV.i]   [*Enter*] Marc Antonio, Gostanzo.

MARC ANTONIO.

    You see how too much wisdom evermore
    Outshoots the truth. You were so forwards still
    To tax my ignorance, my green experience
    In these gray hairs, for giving such advantage
    To my son's spirit that he durst undertake   5
    A secret match so far short of his worth;
    Your son so seasoned with obedience,
    Even from his youth, that all his actions relish
    Nothing but duty and your anger's fear.
    What shall I say to you, if it fall out   10

---

425. *salve your license*] smooth over the liberties you took with Gratiana.
436. *kind*] natural.
437. *hearty policy*] "thorough-going dissimulation" (Parrott).

Second my sad son's feign'd submission,
And see in all points how my brain will answer
His disguis'd grief with a set countenance
Of rage and choler. Now observe and learn
To school your son by me.

Intrant Rinaldo, Valerio, Gratiana.

MARC ANTONIO.   On with your mask.   75
     Here come the other maskers, sir.
RINALDO.   Come on, I say.
     Your father with submission will be calm'd.
     Come on. Down o' your knees.   [*Valerio kneels.*]
GOSTANZO.   Villain, durst thou
     Presume to gull thy father? Dost thou not
     Tremble to see my bent and cloudy brows   80
     Ready to thunder on thy graceless head,
     And with the bolt of my displeasure cut
     The thread of all my living from thy life,
     For taking thus a beggar to thy wife?
VALERIO.

     Father, if that part I have in your blood,   85
     If tears, which so abundantly distil
     Out of my inward eyes, and for a need
     Can drown these outward—[*Aside to* Rinaldo.]   Lend me
         thy handkercher—
     And being indeed as many drops of blood
     Issuing from the creator of my heart,   90
     Be able to beget so much compassion
     Not on my life, but on this lovely dame,
     Whom I hold dearer—
GOSTANZO.   Out upon thee, villain.
MARC ANTONIO.

     Nay, good Gostanzo. Think you are a father.
GOSTANZO.

     I will not hear a word. Out, out upon thee.   95
     Wed without my advice, my love, my knowledge,
     Ay, and a beggar too, a trull, a blowse!

---

75. *S.D. Intrant*] Enter.
97. *a trull, a blowse*] A *trull* is a whore. A *blowse* is a beggar's trull.

His looks to entertain her, now by'r-lady,
Is grown a courtier. For myself, unseen,
Saw when he courted her, embrac'd and kiss'd her,
And I can tell you left not much undone
That was the proper office of your son.   45

MARC ANTONIO.
What world is this?

GOSTANZO.   I told this to Rinaldo,
Advising him to fetch her from my house,
And his young wit not knowing where to lodge her
Unless with you, and saw that could not be
Without some wile, I presently suggested   50
This quaint device, to say she was my son's.
And all this plot, good Marc Antonio,
Flow'd from this fount only to blind your eyes.

MARC ANTONIO.
Out of how sweet a dream have you awak'd me!
By heaven, I durst have laid my part in heaven   55
All had been true; it was so lively handled,
And drawn with such a seeming face of truth.
Your son had cast a perfect veil of grief
Over his face, for his so rash offense
To seal his love with act of marriage   60
Before his father had subscrib'd his choice.
My son (my circumstance lessening the fact)
Entreating me to break the matter to you,
And, joining my effectual persuasions
With your son's penitent submission,   65
Appease your fury, I at first assented,
And now expect their coming to that purpose.

GOSTANZO.
'Twas well. 'Twas well. Seem to believe it still.
Let art end what credulity began.
When they come, suit your words and looks to theirs,   70

53. your] *Collier*; our *Q*.

62. *my circumstance ... fact*] "the circumstance that Marc Antonio
shortly before had believed himself similarly slighted by his son and yet
had not been angry, serves to lessen in his eyes *the fact*, i.e. crime, of Valerio's
deceiving his father" (Parrott).
67. *expect*] await.

RINALDO [*aside to* Gostanzo].

You thought not so last day, when you offer'd her
A twelvemonths' board for one night's lodging with her.

GOSTANZO [*aside*].

Go to, no more of that. Peace, good Rinaldo.   100
It is a fault that only she and you know.

RINALDO [*aside*].

Well, sir, go on, I pray.

GOSTANZO.   Have I, fond wretch,
With utmost care and labor brought thee up,
Ever instructing thee, omitting never
The office of a kind and careful father,   105
To make thee wise and virtuous like thy father,
And hast thou in one act everted all,
Proclaim'd thyself to all the world a fool,
To wed a beggar?

VALERIO.   Father, say not so.

GOSTANZO.

Nay, she's thy own. Here, rise, fool. Take her to thee; 110
Live with her still. I know thou count'st thyself
Happy in soul only in winning her.
Be happy still. Here, take her hand, enjoy her.
Would not a son hazard his father's wrath,
His reputation in the world, his birthright,   115
To have but such a mess of broth as this?

MARC ANTONIO.

Be not so violent, I pray you, good Gostanzo.
Take truce with passion; license your sad son
To speak in his excuse.

GOSTANZO.   What! What excuse?
Can any orator in this case excuse him?   120
What can he say? What can be said of any?

VALERIO.

Alas, sir, hear me. All that I can say

110. S.P. GOSTANZO] *Q* (*corr.*); *not*
in Q (*uncorr.*).

---

107. *everted all*] turned everything upside down.
115–116. *birthright . . . broth*] an allusion to Genesis 25:29–34, where
Esau sold his birthright for a mess of pottage.
121. *What can be . . . any*] what can anyone say.

In my excuse is but to show love's warrant.
GOSTANZO [aside].
    Notable wag.
VALERIO.   I know I have committed
    A great impiety not to move you first   125
    Before the dame I meant to make my wife.
    Consider what I am, yet young and green.
    Behold what she is. Is there not in her,
    Ay, in her very eye, a power to conquer
    Even age itself and wisdom? Call to mind,   130
    Sweet father, what yourself being young have been.
    Think what you may be, for I do not think
    The world so far spent with you but you may
    Look back on such a beauty, and I hope
    To see you young again, and to live long   135
    With young affections. Wisdom makes a man
    Live young for ever, and where is this wisdom
    If not in you? Alas, I know not what
    Rests in your wisdom to subdue affections,
    But I protest it wrought with me so strongly   140
    That I had quite been drown'd in seas of tears,
    Had I not taken hold in happy time
    Of this sweet hand. My heart had been consum'd
    T'a heap of ashes with the flames of love,
    Had it not sweetly been assuag'd and cool'd   145
    With the moist kisses of these sugar'd lips.
GOSTANZO [aside].
    O, puissant wag. What huge large thongs he cuts
    Out of his friend Fortunio's stretching leather.
MARC ANTONIO [aside].
    He knows he does it but to blind my eyes.
GOSTANZO [aside].
    O, excellent! These men will put up anything.   150
VALERIO.
    Had I not had her, I had lost my life,
    Which life indeed I would have lost before

---

125. move] appeal to.
147–148.] "To cut large thongs of other men's leather" was a common
proverb. See Tilley, T 229.

I had displeas'd you, had I not receiv'd it
From such a kind, a wise, and honor'd father.

GOSTANZO [aside].

Notable boy!

VALERIO.   Yet do I here renounce   155
Love, life, and all, rather than one hour longer
Endure to have your love eclipsed from me.

GRATIANA.

O, I can hold no longer. If thy words
Be us'd in earnest, my Valerio,
Thou wound'st my heart, but I know 'tis in jest.   160

GOSTANZO [aside].

No, I'll be sworn she has her lyripoop too.

GRATIANA.

Didst thou not swear to love me spite of father
And all the world, that nought should sever us
But death itself?

VALERIO.   I did, but if my father
Will have his son forsworn, upon his soul   165
The blood of my black perjury shall lie,
For I will seek his favor though I die.

GOSTANZO.

No, no. Live still my son. Thou well shalt know,
I have a father's heart. Come, join your hands.
Still keep thy vows, and live together still,   170
Till cruel death set foot betwixt you both.

VALERIO.

O speak you this in earnest?

GOSTANZO.   Ay, by heaven.

VALERIO.

And never to recall it?

GOSTANZO.   Not till death.

RINALDO.

Excellent sir, you have done like yourself.
What would you more, Valerio?

VALERIO.   Worshipful father!   175

---

161. *she ... lyripoop*] "has her wits about her. The word *lyripoop*, i.e. a
scarf or hood (lyripipium) worn by one who had taken a university degree,
was used figuratively to denote first learning, then wit or common sense"
(Parrott).

RINALDO.

    Come, sir, come you in, and celebrate your joys.

Exeunt all save the old men.

GOSTANZO.

    O Marc Antonio,

    Had I not arm'd you with an expectation,

    Would not this make you pawn your very soul

    The wench had been my son's wife?

MARC ANTONIO.   Yes, by heaven.   180

    A knavery thus effected might deceive

    A wiser man than I, for I, alas,

    Am no good politician. Plain believing,

    Simple honesty, is my policy still.

GOSTANZO.

    The visible marks of folly, honesty   185

    And quick credulity, his younger brother.

    I tell you, Marc Antonio, there is much

    In that young boy, my son.

MARC ANTONIO.   Not much honesty,

    If I may speak without offense to his father.

GOSTANZO.

    O God, you cannot please me better, sir.   190

    H'as honesty enough to serve his turn;

    The less honesty ever the more wit.

    But go you home, and use your daughter kindly.

    Meantime I'll school your son, and do you still

    Dissemble what you know. Keep off your son.   195

    The wench at home must still be my son's wife.

    Remember that, and be you blinded still.

MARC ANTONIO.

    You must remember, too, to let your son

    Use his accustom'd visitations,

    Only to blind my eyes.

GOSTANZO.   He shall not fail.   200

    But still take you heed, have a vigilant eye

    On that sly child of mine, for by this light,

    He'll be too bold with your son's forehead else.

MARC ANTONIO.

    Well, sir, let me alone. I'll bear a brain.   *Exeunt.*

---

204. *I'll . . . brain*] a proverb meaning *I'll watch out*. See Tilley, B 596.

Enter Valerio, Rinaldo.

VALERIO.

Come, they are gone.

RINALDO.   Gone? They were far gone here.   205

VALERIO.

Gull'd I my father, or gull'd he himself?

Thou told'st him Gratiana was my wife,

I have confess'd it, he has pardon'd it.

RINALDO.

Nothing more true, enow can witness it.

And therefore when he comes to learn the truth   210

(As certainly, for all these sly disguises,

Time will strip Truth into her nakedness),

Thou hast good plea against him to confess

The honor'd action, and to claim his pardon.

VALERIO.

'Tis true, for all was done, he deeply swore,   215

Out of his heart.

RINALDO.   He has much faith the whiles

That swore a thing so quite against his heart.

VALERIO.

Why, this is policy.

RINALDO.   Well, see you repair

To Gratiana daily, and enjoy her

In her true kind. And now we must expect   220

The resolute and ridiculous divorce

Cornelio hath sued against his wedlock.

VALERIO.

I think it be not so; the ass dotes on her.

RINALDO.

It is too true, and thou shalt answer it

For setting such debate 'twixt man and wife.   225

See, we shall see the solemn manner of it.

Enter Cornelio, Dariotto, Claudio, Notary, Page, Gazetta, Bellanora,
Gratiana.

---

209. *enow*] persons enough.
214. *honor'd action*] the marriage. Rinaldo speaks in legal terms.
220. *In . . . kind*] as a wife.

BELLANORA.

Good Signor Cornelio, let us poor gentlewomen entreat you
to forbear.

CORNELIO.

Talk no more to me. I'll not be made cuckold in my own
house. Notary, read me the divorce.   230

GAZETTA.

My dear Cornelio, examine the cause better before you
condemn me.

CORNELIO.

Sing to me no more, siren, for I will hear thee no more. I
will take no compassion on thee.

PAGE.

Good Signor Cornelio, be not too mankind against your 235
wife. Say y'are a cuckold (as the best that is may be so at a
time) will you make a trumpet of your own horns?

CORNELIO.

Go to, sir, y'are a rascal. I'll give you a fee for pleading
for her one day. Notary, do you your office.

VALERIO.

Go to, signor. Look better to your wife, and be better 240
advised before you grow to this extremity.

CORNELIO.

Extremity? Go to, I deal but too mercifully with her.
If I should use extremity with her, I might hang her and
her copesmate, my drudge here. How say you, Master
Notary, might I not do it by law?   245

NOTARY.

Not hang 'em, but you may bring them both to a white
sheet.

CORNELIO.

Nay, by the mass, they have had too much of the sheet
already.

NOTARY.

And besides you may set capital letters on their foreheads. 250

---

235. *mankind*] furious, fierce.
244. *copesmate*] lover.
246–247. *white sheet*] worn as a sign of public penance by adulterers.
250. *capital letters*] bound on the foreheads of offenders indicating their
crime.

CORNELIO.

What's that to the capital letter that's written in mind?
I say for all your law, Master Notary, that I may hang 'em.
May I not hang him that robs me of mine honor as well
as he that robs me of my horse?

NOTARY.

No, sir. Your horse is a chattel.   255

CORNELIO.

So is honor. A man may buy it with his penny, and if I
may hang a man for stealing my horse (as I say), much
more for robbing me of my honor. For why? If my horse
be stolen, it may be my own fault. For why? Either the
stable is not strong enough, or the pasture not well fenced, 260
or watched, or so forth. But for your wife that keeps the
stable of your honor, let her be locked in a brazen tower,
let Argus himself keep her, yet can you never be secure of
your honor. For why? She can run through all with her
serpent noddle. Besides, you may hang a lock upon your 265
horse, and so can you not upon your wife.

RINALDO.

But I pray you, sir, what are the presumptions on which
you would build this divorce?

CORNELIO.

Presumption enough, sir. For besides their intercourse,
or commerce of glances that passed betwixt this cockerel- 270
drone and her, at my table the last Sunday night at supper,
their winks, their becks—*Dieu garde*—their treads o'the toe
(as, by heaven, I swear she trod once upon my toe instead

---

251. *in mind*] within the mind itself as opposed to outside, on the
forehead.

261–262. *keeps the stable*] "'The phrase to *keep one's stables* was a familiar
phrase in Shakespeare's day; and meant to keep a personal watch over one's
wife's or one's mistress' chastity'—Ingleby, *Shakespeare Hermeneutics*, p. 77"
(Parrott).

262. *brazen tower*] as was Danaë, whom Zeus visited in a shower of gold.

263. *Argus*] Argus Panoptes (the all-seeing), who had a hundred eyes.
See Ovid, *Metamorphoses*, I, 677–723.

265. *serpent noddle*] snake's head, referring to woman's ability to deceive
her husband.

270–271. *cockerel-drone*] young cock who will not work.

272. *Dieu garde*] God help us.

of his), this is chiefly to be noted: the same night she
would needs lie alone, and the same night her dog barked. 275
Did not you hear him, Valerio?

VALERIO.

And understand him too, I'll be sworn of a book.

CORNELIO.

Why, very good. If these be not manifest presumptions
now, let the world be judge. Therefore without more
ceremony, Master Notary, pluck out your instrument.   280

NOTARY.

I will, sir, if there be no remedy.

CORNELIO.

Have you made it strong in law, Master Notary? Have
you put in words enough?

NOTARY.

I hope so, sir; it has taken me a whole skin of parchment,
you see.   285

CORNELIO.

Very good, and is egress and regress in?

NOTARY.

I'll warrant you, sir, it is *forma juris.*

CORNELIO.

Is there no hole to be found in the orthography?

NOTARY.

None in the world, sir.

CORNELIO.

You have written *Sunt* with an *S*, have you not?   290

NOTARY.

Yes, that I have.

CORNELIO.

You have done the better for quietness' sake. And are
none of the authentical dashes over the head left out?
If there be, Master Notary, an error will lie out.

---

280. *pluck . . . instrument*] legal instrument, but also a bawdy pun.
286. *egress and regress*] part of a legal phrase, "ingress, egress, and regress,"
meaning the right to go out and come back, but also with bawdy overtones.
287. *forma juris*] in the proper legal form.
290. written . . . an *S*] instead of a bawdy *C.*
293. *authentical dashes*] legal flourishes, but also knocks on the head.
294. *lie out*] "Stretch out, extend" (*OED*).

NOTARY.

Not for a dash over head, sir, I warrant you, if I should 295
oversee. I have seen that tried in Butiro and Caseo, in
Butler and Cason's case, *decimo sexto* of Duke Anonimo.

RINALDO.

Y'ave gotten a learned notary, Signor Cornelio,

CORNELIO.

He's a shrewd fellow indeed. I had as lief have his head
in a matter of felony or treason as any notary in Florence. 300
Read out, Master Notary. Hearken you, mistress;
gentlemen, mark, I beseech you.

OMNES.

We will all mark you, sir, I warrant you.

NOTARY.

I think it would be something tedious to read all, and
therefore, gentlemen, the sum is this: That you, Signor 305
Cornelio, gentleman, for divers and sundry weighty and
mature considerations you especially moving, specifying
all the particulars of your wife's enormities in a schedule
hereunto annexed, the transcript whereof is in your own
tenure, custody, occupation, and keeping: That for these, 310
the aforesaid premises, I say, you renounce, disclaim, and
discharge Gazetta from being your leeful or your lawful wife:
And that you eftsoons divide, disjoin, separate, remove, and
finally eloign, sequester, and divorce her, from your bed
and your board: That you forbid her all access, repair, 315
egress or regress to your person or persons, mansion or
mansions, dwellings, habitations, remanences, or abodes, or
to any shop, cellar, sollar, easement's chamber, dormer, and
so forth, now in the tenure, custody, occupation, or keeping
of the said Cornelio; notwithstanding all former contracts, 320
convenants, bargains, conditions, agreements, compacts,

---

296. *Butiro and Caseo*] Latin for butter and cheese (*butyrum et caseus*).

297. *decimo . . . Anonimo*] the sixteenth chapter (or paragraph) of Duke
Anonymous. A usual form of bibliographical citation in the Renaissance.

299. *have his head*] have his legal advice; but decapitation was also the
usual punishment for treason.

308. *schedule*] appendix, separate paper.

313. *eftsoons*] moreover.

318. *sollar, easement's chamber, dormer*] loft or attic, toilet, bedroom.

promises, vows, affiances, assurances, bonds, bills, inden-
tures, polldeeds, deeds of gift, defeasances, feoffments,
endowments, vouchers, double vouchers, privy entries,
actions, declarations, explications, rejoinders, surrejoinders, 325
rights, interests, demands, claims, or titles whatsoever,
heretofore betwixt the one and the other party, or parties,
being had, made, passed, covenanted, and agreed, from the
beginning of the world till the day of the date hereof. Given
the seventeenth of November, fifteen hundred and so forth. 330
Here, sir, you must set to your hand.

CORNELIO.

What else, Master Notary? I am resolute, i'faith.

GAZETTA.

Sweet husband, forbear.

CORNELIO.

Avoid, I charge thee in name of this divorce. Thou mightst
have looked to it in time, yet this I will do for thee. If thou 335
canst spy out any other man that thou wouldst cuckold,
thou shalt have my letter to him. I can do no more. More
ink, Master Notary. I write my name at large.

NOTARY.

Here is more, sir.

CORNELIO.

Ah, ass, that thou could not know thy happiness till thou 340
hadst lost it. How now? My nose bleed? Shall I write in
blood? What, only three drops? 'Sfoot, this's ominous. I
will not set my hand to't now, certain. Master Notary,
I like not this abodement. I will defer the setting to of my
hand till the next court day. Keep the divorce, I pray you, 345
and the woman in your house together.

---

322. *affiances*] pledges.
323. *polldeeds*] deeds made by one party only, which are therefore polled
or cut even, not indented.
323. *defeasances*] paper listing conditions which make the deed it is
attached to void.
323. *feoffments*] deeds conveying "corporeal hereditaments" (*OED*).
330. *fifteen . . . forth*] an important indication of the date when the play
was written. It was first published in 1605. See Introduction, pp. xviii–xix.
337. *my letter*] of recommendation.
338. *at large*] either in large letters or in full.
344. *abodement*] omen.

OMNES.

Burn the divorce, burn the divorce.

CORNELIO.

Not so, sir. It shall not serve her turn. Master Notary,
keep it at your peril, and gentlemen, you may be gone,
o' God's name. What have you to do to flock about me   350
thus? I am neither howlet nor cuckoo. Gentlewomen, for
God's sake, meddle with your own cases. It is not fit you
should haunt these public assemblies.

OMNES.

Well, farewell, Cornelio.

VALERIO.

Use the gentlewoman kindly, Master Notary.   355

NOTARY.

As mine own wife, I assure you, sir.

          Exeunt [all but Claudio *and* Cornelio].

CLAUDIO.

Signor Cornelio, I cannot but in kindness tell you that
Valerio, by counsel of Rinaldo, hath whispered all this
jealousy into your ears. Not that he knew any just cause
in your wife, but only to be revenged on you for the gull 360
you put upon him when you drew him with his glory to
touch the theorbo.

CORNELIO.

May I believe this?

CLAUDIO.

As I am a gentleman. And if this accident of your nose
had not fallen out, I would have told you this before you 365
set to your hand.

CORNELIO.

It may well be. Yet have I cause enough
To perfect my divorce. But it shall rest
Till I conclude it with a counterbuff
Given to these noble rascals. Claudio, thanks.   370
What comes of this, watch but my brain a little,

---

348. Master] *Parrott*; M. *Q.*   358. Valerio] *Collier*; Balerio *Q.*
356. S.P. NOTARY] *Shepherd, after*
Collier; not in Q.

---

351. *neither . . . cuckoo*] Both are attacked by other birds.

And ye shall see if like two parts in me
I leave not both these gullers' wits imbrier'd.
Now I perceive well where the wild wind sits,
Here's gull for gull and wits at war with wits.   *Exeunt.* 375

[*Finis Actus Quarti.*]

[V.i]   Rinaldo, *solus.*

RINALDO.

Fortune, the great commandress of the world,
Hath divers ways to advance her followers.
To some she gives honor without deserving,
To other some, deserving without honor,
Some wit, some wealth, and some wit without wealth,   5
Some wealth without wit, some, nor wit nor wealth
But good smock-faces, or some qualities
By nature without judgment, with the which
They live in sensual acceptation,
And make show only, without touch of substance.   10
My fortune is to win renown by gulling
Gostanzo, Dariotto, and Cornelio,
All which suppose, in all their different kinds,
Their wits entire, and in themselves no piece.
All at one blow, my helmet yet unbruis'd,   15
I have unhors'd, laid flat on earth for gulls.
Now in what taking˘poor Cornelio is
Betwixt his large divorce and no divorce,
I long to see, and what he will resolve.
I lay my life he cannot chew his meat,   20
And looks much like an ape had swallowed pills,
And all this comes of bootless jealousy.

---

372. *like . . . me*] "as if they were parts of myself, I will have so much control over them."
[V.i]
6–9. *nor wit . . . acceptation*] Some people have neither wit nor wealth, only pretty faces, yet our senses approve of them (*sensual acceptation*). *Smock faces* were actually "pale, smooth, and effeminate" (*OED*).
14. *piece*] fragment. In opposition to *entire* in the same line.
17. *taking*] disturbed state of mind.
22. *bootless*] useless, unprofitable.

And see, where bootless jealousy appears.

Enter Cornelio.

I'll bourd him straight. —How now, Cornelio,
Are you resolv'd on the divorce or no?   25

CORNELIO.

What's that to you? Look to your own affairs;
The time requires it. Are not you engag'd
In some bonds forfeit for Valerio?

RINALDO.

Yes, what of that?

CORNELIO.   Why, so am I myself,
And both our dangers great. He is arrested   30
On a recognizance by a usuring slave.

RINALDO.

Arrested? I am sorry with my heart.
It is a matter may import me much.
May not our bail suffice to free him, think you?

CORNELIO.

I think it may, but I must not be seen in't,   35
Nor would I wish you, for we both are parties,
And liker far to bring ourselves in trouble,
Than bear him out. I have already made
Means to the officers to sequester him
In private for a time till some in secret   40
Might make his father understand his state,
Who would perhaps take present order for him
Rather than suffer him t'endure the shame
Of his imprisonment. Now, would you but go
And break the matter closely to his father   45
(As you can wisely do't), and bring him to him,
This were the only way to save his credit,
And to keep off a shrewd blow from ourselves.

RINALDO.

I know his father will be mov'd past measure.

---

24. *bourd*] make fun of, mock.
31. *recognizance*] bond or obligation; in this case, a debt.
42. *take present order*] secure his immediate release.
48. *shrewd*] grievous, formidable.

CORNELIO.

Nay, if you stand on such nice ceremonies,   50
Farewell our substance. Extreme diseases
Ask extreme remedies. Better he should storm
Some little time than we be beat forever
Under the horrid shelter of a prison.

RINALDO.

Where is the place?

CORNELIO.   'Tis at the Half Moon Tavern.   55
Haste, for the matter will abide no stay.

RINALDO.

Heaven send my speed be equal with my haste.   *Exit.*

CORNELIO.

Go, shallow scholar, you that make all gulls,
You that can out-see clear-eyed jealousy,
Yet make this sleight a millstone, where your brain   60
Sticks in the midst amaz'd. This gull to him
And to his fellow guller shall become
More bitter than their baiting of my humor.
Here at this tavern shall Gostanzo find
Fortunio, Dariotto, Claudio,   65
And amongst them, the ringleader, his son,
His husband, and his Saint Valerio—
That knows not of what fashion dice are made,
Nor ever yet look'd towards a red lettice
(Thinks his blind sire), at drinking and at dice—   70
With all their wenches, and at full discover
His own gross folly and his son's distempers.
And both shall know (although I be no scholar)
Yet I have thus much Latin, as to say
Jam sumus ergo pares.   *Exit.*   75

---

50. *nice*] fastidious.

52–54. *Better . . . prison*] The image is of a ship beaten by the wind into a harbor *horrid* (in the Latin sense of "bristling") with rocks.

60–61. *millstone . . . amaz'd.*] variant of the proverb "to see into a millstone" which according to Tilley (M 965) is "A claim to acuteness, often used ironically."

69. *red lettice*] red lattice; usual sign for a tavern.

75. *Jam . . . pares*] "So now we're even." Parrott notes that the phrase occurs three times in Martial II, 18.

[V.ii]
Enter Valerio, Fortunio, Claudio, Page, Gratiana, Gazetta, Bellanora.
A Drawer *or two, setting a table.*

VALERIO.
Set me the table here. We will shift rooms
To see if Fortune will shift chances with us.
Sit, ladies, sit. Fortunio, place thy wench,
And Claudio, place you Dariotto's mistress.
I wonder where that neat, spruce slave becomes.   5
I think he was some barber's son, by th' mass.
'Tis such a picked fellow, not a hair
About his whole bulk but it stands in print.
Each pin hath his due place, not any point
But hath his perfect tie, fashion, and grace.   10
A thing whose soul is specially employ'd
In knowing where best gloves, best stockings, waistcoats
Curiously wrought are sold, sacks milliners' shops
For all new tires and fashions, and can tell ye
What new devices of all sorts there are,   15
And that there is not in the whole Rialto
But one new-fashion'd waistcoat, or one nightcap,
One pair of gloves pretty or well perfum'd,
And from a pair of gloves of half a crown
To twenty crowns, will to a very scute   20
Smell out the price. And for these womanly parts
He is esteem'd a witty gentleman.

Enter Dariotto.

FORTUNIO.
See where he comes.

---

5. *where . . . becomes*] what has become of.

7. *picked*] trimmed, neat, fashionable, but also with a possible play on baldness.

8. *in print*] in perfect order.

9. *point*] a tag or lace used to attach one piece of clothing to another, usually the hose to the doublet.

14. *tires*] attires.

16. *Rialto*] the exchange or market in Venice, which Chapman shifts to Florence.

20. *scute*] "used vaguely for a coin of small value" (*OED*).

DARIOTTO.   God save you, lovely ladies.
VALERIO.

    Ay, well said, lovely Paris. Your walleye
    Must ever first be gloating on men's wives.   25
    You think to come upon us, being half drunk,
    And so to part the freshest man among us,
    But you shall overtake us, I'll be sworn.
DARIOTTO.

    Tush, man, where are your dice? Let's fall to them.
CLAUDIO.

    We have been at 'em. Drawer, call for more.   30
VALERIO.

    First let's have wine. Dice have no perfect edge
    Without the liquid whetstone of the syrup.
FORTUNIO.

    True, and to welcome Dariotto's lateness,
    He shall (unpledg'd) carouse one crowned cup
    To all these ladies' health.
DARIOTTO.   I am well pleas'd.   35
VALERIO.

    Come on, let us vary our sweet time
    With sundry exercises. Boy! Tobacco.
    And, drawer, you must get us music too.
    Call's in a cleanly noise, the slaves grow lousy.
DRAWER.

    You shall have such as we can get you, sir.   *Exit.* 40
DARIOTTO.

    Let's have some dice, I pray thee; they are cleanly.
VALERIO.

    Page, let me see that leaf.
PAGE.   It is not leaf, sir.
    'Tis pudding-cane tobacco.

---

   34. *unpledg'd*] drink alone, without an answering pledge or toast from one of the company.
   34. *crowned*] full to the brim.
   39. *noise*] band of musicians.
   42. *leaf*] leaf tobacco.
   43. *pudding-cane*] "tobacco rolled into a tight stick or cane in the shape of a sausage (*pudding*), which has to be shredded by the knife before smoking" (Parrott).

VALERIO.   But I mean
    Your linstock, sir. What leaf is that, I pray?
PAGE.
    I pray you see, sir, for I cannot read.   45
VALERIO.
    'Sfoot, a rank, stinking satire. This had been
    Enough to have poison'd every man of us.
DARIOTTO.
    And now you speak of that, my boy once lighted
    A pipe of cane tobacco with a piece
    Of a vild ballad, and I'll swear I had   50
    A singing in my head a whole week after.
VALERIO.
    Well, th'old verse is, *A potibus incipe io-c-um.*

                Enter Drawer *with wine and a cup.*

VALERIO.
    Drawer, fill out this gentleman's carouse,
    And harden him for our society.
DARIOTTO.
    Well, ladies, here is to your honor'd healths.   55
FORTUNIO.
    What, Dariotto, without hat or knee?
VALERIO.
    Well said, Fortunio. O, y'are a rare courtier.
    Your knee, good signor, I beseech your knee.
DARIOTTO.
    Nay, pray you. Let's take it by degrees,
    Valerio. On our feet first, for this   60
    Will bring's too soon upon our knees.
VALERIO.   Sir, there
    Are no degrees of order in a tavern.
    Here you must, I charg'd ye, run all ahead.
    'Slight, courtier, down.

52. *potibus*] *Q* (*corr.*); *petibus Q*.
(*uncorr.*).

---

    44. *linstock*] a forked stick used to hold the tinder which fired a cannon;
here used for the leaf of an old book used to light a pipe.
    52. *A potibus incipe io-c-um*] "Let the drinks begin the joking."

I hope you are no elephant. You have joints?   65
DARIOTTO.
    Well, sir, here's to the ladies, on my knees.   *He kneels.*
VALERIO.
    I'll be their pledge.

            Enter Gostanzo *and* Rinaldo [*unseen by the others*].

FORTUNIO.   Not yet, Valerio.
    This he must drink unpledg'd.
VALERIO.
    He shall not. I will give him this advantage.
GOSTANZO.
    How now, what's here? Are these the officers?   70
RINALDO [*aside*].
    'Slight, I would all were well.

            Enter Cornelio [*unseen by the others*].

VALERIO.   Here is his pledge.
    Here's to our common friend Cornelio's health.
DARIOTTO.
    Health to Gazetta, poison to her husband.
CORNELIO [*aside*].
    Excellent guests; these are my daily guests.
VALERIO.
    Drawer, make even th'impartial scales of justice.   75
    Give it to Claudio, and from him fill round.
    Come, Dariotto, set me. Let the rest
    Come in when they have done the ladies right.
GOSTANZO.
    Set me! Do you know what belongs to setting?
RINALDO [*aside*].
    What a dull slave was I to be thus gull'd.   80
CORNELIO [*aside to* Rinaldo].
    Why, Rinald, what meant you to intrap your friend,

66. S.D. *He kneels*] *this edn.*; *after*   73. S.P. DARIOTTO] *Parrott*; *Clau. Q*.
l. 73 in Q.   77. the] *Parrott*; mee *Q*.

    65. *elephant*] Elephants were believed to have no joints and so could not
kneel.
    77. *set me*] set me a stake, make me a bet.

And bring his father to this spectacle?
You are a friend indeed.

RINALDO.   'Tis very good, sir.
Perhaps my friend, or I, before we part,
May make even with you.

FORTUNIO.   Come, let's set him round.   85

VALERIO.
Do so. At all! A plague upon these dice.
Another health. 'Sfoot, I shall have no luck
Till I be drunk. Come on, here's to the comfort
The cavalier, my father, should take in me
If he now saw me, and would do me right.   90

FORTUNIO.
I'll pledge it, and his health, Valerio.

GOSTANZO.
Here's a good husband.

RINALDO.   I pray you have patience, sir.

VALERIO.
Now have at all, an 'twere a thousand pound.

GOSTANZO [coming forward].
Hold sir. I bar the dice.

VALERIO.   What, sir, are you there?
Fill's a fresh pottle. By this light, Sir Knight,   95
You shall do right.

                    Enter Marc Antonio.

GOSTANZO.   O, thou ungracious villain.

VALERIO.
Come, come, we shall have you now thunder forth
Some of your thrifty sentences, as gravely:
"For as much, Valerius, as everything has time, and a

97. S.P. VALERIO] Shepherd; not in
Q.

_____

85. set him round] all bet against him.
86. At all] i.e., Valerio will play for any sums the others may choose to
risk against him.
93. an] even if.
95. pottle] A pottle was originally a half gallon.
98. thrifty sentences] sententia, wise sayings, aphorisms.
99–100. everything . . . two] a common proverb. See Tilley, E 121:
"Everything has an end and a pudding has two."

pudding has two, yet ought not satisfaction to swerve so 100
much from defalcation of well-disposed people, as that
indemnity should prejudice what security doth insinuate."
A trial, yet once again!

MARC ANTONIO.
　　Here's a good sight. Y'are well encounter'd, sir.
　　Did not I tell you you'd o'ershoot yourself   105
　　With too much wisdom?

VALERIO.　　　　　　　　Sir, your wisest do so.
　　Fill the old man some wine.

GOSTANZO.　　　　　　　Here's a good infant.

MARC ANTONIO.
　　Why, sir? Alas, I'll wager with your wisdom
　　His consorts drew him to it, for of himself
　　He is both virtuous, bashful, innocent,   110
　　Comes not at city, knows no city art,
　　But plies your husbandry, dares not view a wench.

VALERIO.
　　Father, he comes upon you.

GOSTANZO.　　　　　　　Here's a son.

MARC ANTONIO.
　　Whose wife is Gratiana now, I pray?

GOSTANZO.
　　Sing your old song no more. Your brain's too short   115
　　To reach into these policies.

MARC ANTONIO.　　　　　　'Tis true,
　　Mine eye's soon blinded, and yourself would say so,
　　If you knew all. Where lodg'd your son last night?
　　Do you know that with all your policy?

GOSTANZO.
　　You'll say he lodg'd with you. And did not I   120
　　Foretell you all this must for color sake
　　Be brought about, only to blind your eyes?

MARC ANTONIO.
　　By heaven, I chanc'd this morn, I know not why,
　　To pass by Gratiana's bedchamber,

---

　　101. *defalcation*] diminution, curtailment. The passage, of course, does not
make any sense.
　　103. *trial*] bet, that is, another round of the dice.
　　113. *comes upon you*] attacks you suddenly, by surprise.

And whom saw I fast by her naked side 125
But your Valerio.

GOSTANZO.   Had you not warning given?
Did not I bid you watch my courtier well,
Or he would set a crest o' your son's head?

MARC ANTONIO.
That was not all, for by them on a stool
My son sat laughing to see you so gull'd. 130

GOSTANZO.
'Tis too, too plain.

MARC ANTONIO.   Why, sir, do you suspect it
The more for that?

GOSTANZO.   Suspect it? Is there any
So gross a wittol as, if 'twere his wife,
Would sit by her so tamely?

MARC ANTONIO.   Why not, sir,
To blind my eyes?

GOSTANZO.   Well, sir, I was deceiv'd, 135
But I shall make it prove a dear deceit
To the deceiver.

RINALDO.   Nay, sir, let's not have
A new infliction set on an old fault.
He did confess his fault upon his knees.
You pardon'd it, and swore 'twas from your heart. 140

GOSTANZO.
Swore, a great piece of work! The wretch shall know
I have a daughter here to give my land to.
I'll give my daughter all. The prodigal
Shall not have one poor house to hide his head in.

FORTUNIO.
I humbly thank you, sir, and vow all duty 145
My life can yield you.

GOSTANZO.   Why are you so thankful?

FORTUNIO.
For giving to your daughter all your lands,
Who is my wife, and so you gave them me.

GOSTANZO.
Better and better!

---

128. *crest*] coxcomb, that is, make a fool of him.

FORTUNIO.   Pray, sir, be not mov'd.
You drew me kindly to your house, and gave me   150
Access to woo your daughter, whom I lov'd,
And since (by honor'd marriage) made my wife.

GOSTANZO.
Now all my choler fly out in your wits.
Good tricks of youth, i'faith, no indecorum,
Knight's son, knight's daughter. Marc Antonio,   155
Give me your hand. There is no remedy.
Marriage is ever made by destiny.

RINALDO.
Silence, my masters. Now here all are pleas'd,
Only but Cornelio, who lacks but persuasion
To reconcile himself to his fair wife.   160
Good sir, will you (of all men our best speaker)
Persuade him to receive her into grace?

GOSTANZO.
That I will gladly, and he shall be rul'd. Good Cornelio,
I have heard of your wayward jealousy, and I must tell
you plain as a friend, y'are an ass. You must pardon me; 165
I knew your father.

RINALDO.
Then you must pardon him, indeed, sir.

GOSTANZO.
Understand me: put case Dariotto loved your wife,
whereby you would seem to refuse her. Would you
desire to have such a wife as no man could love but 170
yourself?

MARC ANTONIO.
Answer but that, Cornelio.

GOSTANZO.
Understand me: say Dariotto hath kissed your wife, or
performed other offices of that nature, whereby they
did converse together at bed and at board, as friends 175
may seem to do.—

MARC ANTONIO.
Mark but the "now understand me."

153.] "Now all my anger passes away because of your wit."

GOSTANZO.

Yet if there come no proofs but that her actions were
cleanly, or in discreet private, why, 'twas a sign of
modesty. And will you blow the horn yourself, when you 180
may keep it to yourself? Go to, you are a fool;
understand me!

VALERIO.

Do understand him, Cornelio.

GOSTANZO.

Nay, Cornelio, I tell you again, I knew your father.
He was a wise gentleman, and so was your mother. Methinks 185
I see her yet, a lusty, stout woman, bore great children.
You were the very scoundrel of 'em all, but let that pass.
As for your mother, she was wise. A most flippant tongue
she had, and could set out her tail with as good grace as
any she in Florence, come cut and long-tail, and she was 190
honest enough too. But yet, by your leave, she would tickle
Dob now and then, as well as the best on 'em. By Jove, it's
true, Cornelio. I speak it not to flatter you. Your father
knew it well enough, and would he do as you do, think you?
Set rascals to undermine her, or look to her water (as 195
they say)? No, when he saw 'twas but her humor (for
his own quietness' sake) he made a back-door to his house
for convenience, got a bell to his fore-door, and had an
odd fashion in ringing, by which she and her maid knew
him, and would stand talking to his next neighbor to prolong 200
time, that all things might be rid cleanly out o'the way
before he came, for the credit of his wife. This was wisdom
now, for a man's own quiet.

MARC ANTONIO.

Here was a man, Cornelio.

GOSTANZO.

What, I say! Young men think old men are fools, but 205
old men know young men are fools.

---

190. *come cut and long-tail*] a proverb meaning "Come one and all, long
tail or bobtail." See Tilley, C 938.
191–192. *tickle Dob*] carry on extra-marital affairs (?).
205–206.] The entire speech is a common proverb. See the *Oxford
Dictionary of English Proverbs* (Oxford, 1935), pp. 608–609.

CORNELIO.

Why, hark you, you two knights. Do you think I will
forsake Gazetta?

GOSTANZO.

And will you not?

CORNELIO.

Why, there's your wisdom. Why did I make show of 210
divorce, think you?

MARC ANTONIO.

Pray you why, sir?

CORNELIO.

Only to bridle her stout stomach, and how did I draw
on the color for my divorce? I did train the woodcock
Dariotto into the net, drew him to my house, gave him 215
opportunity with my wife (as you say my father dealt
with his wife's friends) only to train him in; let him alone
with my wife in her bedchamber, and sometimes found
him abed with her, and went my way back again softly,
only to draw him into the pit.   220

GOSTANZO.

This was well handled indeed, Cornelio.

MARC ANTONIO.

Ay marry, sir. Now I commend your wisdom.

CORNELIO.

Why, if I had been so minded as you think, I could have
flung his pantable down the stairs, or done him some
other disgrace. But I winked at it, and drew on the 225
good fool more and more, only to bring him within my
compass.

GOSTANZO.

Why, this was policy in grain.

CORNELIO.

And now shall the world see I am as wise as my
father.   230

---

213. *bridle . . . stomach*] put a check on her innate sexuality.
213–214. *draw on the color*] make a pretense.
214. *train*] lure.
214. *woodcock*] simpleton.
224. *pantable*] slipper.
228. *in grain*] downright, genuine.

VALERIO.

    Is't come to this? Then will I make a speech in praise of this
reconcilement, including therein the praise and honor of
the most fashionable and authentical HORN. Stand close,
gentles, and be silent.   *He gets into a chair.*

GOSTANZO.

    Come on. Let's hear his wit in this potable humor.   235

VALERIO.

    The course of the world (like the life of man) is said to
be divided into several ages. As we into infancy, child-
hood, youth, and so forward to old age, so the world
into the golden age, the silver, the brass, the iron, the
leaden, the wooden, and now into this present age, 240
which we term the *horned age*. Not that but former ages
have enjoyed this benefit as well as our times, but that
in ours it is more common, and nevertheless precious.
It is said that in the golden age of the world the use of
gold was not then known: an argument of the simplicity 245
of that age. Lest therefore succeeding ages should hereafter
impute the same fault to us which we lay upon the first age,
that we, living in the horned age of the world, should not
understand the use, the virtue, the honor, and the very
royalty of the horn, I will in brief sound the praises 250
thereof that they who are already in possession of it may
bear their heads aloft as being proud of such lofty accouter-
ments, and they that are but in possibility may be ravished
with a desire to be in possession.

    A trophy so honorable and unmatchably powerful that it 255
is able to raise any man from a beggar to an emperor's
fellow, a duke's fellow, a nobleman's fellow, alderman's
fellow; so glorious that it deserves to be worn (by most
opinions) in the most conspicuous place about a man. For
what worthier crest can you bear than the horn, which if it 260
might be seen with our mortal eyes, what a wonderful
spectacle would there be, and how highly they would ravish
the beholders? But their substance is incorporal, not

---

    235. *potable*] The *OED* cites this as the only example of the rare use of the
term meaning "appropriate to drinking." More probably it means
drunken.

falling under sense, nor mixed of the gross concretion of
elements, but a quintessence beyond them, a spiritual 265
essence, invisible and everlasting.

And this hath been the cause that many men have called
their being in question, whether there be such a thing *in
rerum natura*, or not, because they are not to be seen; as
though nothing were that were not to be seen! Who ever 270
saw the wind? Yet what wonderful effects are seen of it!
It drives the clouds, yet no man sees it. It rocks the house,
bears down trees, castles, steeples, yet who sees it? In
like sort does your horn. It swells the forehead, yet none
sees it. It rocks the cradle, yet none sees it. So that you 275
plainly perceive sense is no judge of essence. The moon to
any man's sense seems to be horned, yet who knows not
the moon to be ever perfectly round? So likewise your heads
seem ever to be round, when indeed they are oftentimes
horned. For their original, it is unsearchable. Natural they 280
are not, for where is beast born with horns, more than with
teeth? Created they were not, for *ex nihilo nihil fit*. Then will
you ask me, how came they into the world? I know not,
but I am sure women brought them into this part of the
world, howsoever some doctors are of opinion that they 285
came in with the Devil. And not unlike, for as the Devil
brought sin into the world, but the woman brought it to the
man, so it may very well be that the Devil brought horns
into the world, but the woman brought them to the man.

For their power, it is general over the world. No nation 290
so barbarous, no country so proud, but doth equal homage
to the horn. Europa, when she was carried through the sea
by the Saturnian bull, was said (for fear of falling) to
have held by the horn, and what is this but a plain showing
to us, that all Europe, which took name from that Europa, 295
should likewise hold by the horn. So that I say it is
universal over the face of the world, general over the

---

281. where] *Collier*; there *Q*.   295. Europe] *Collier*; *Europa Q*.

268–269. *in rerum natura*] in the nature of things.
282. *ex . . . fit*] nothing is made from nothing.
293. *Saturnian bull*] Zeus, son of Saturn, who disguised as a bull, kid-
napped Europa and carried her off to Crete.

face of Europe, and common over the face of this country. What city, what town, what village, what street, nay, what house, can quit itself of this prerogative? I have read that 300 the lion once made a proclamation through all the forest, that all horned beasts should depart forthwith upon pain of death. If this proclamation should be made through our forest, Lord, what pressing, what running, what flying would there be even from all the parts of it! He that had but 305 a bunch of flesh in his head would away, and some, foolishly fearful, would imagine the shadow of his ears to be horns. Alas, how desert would this forest be left!

To conclude: for their force it is irrevitable, for were they not irrevitable, then might either properness of 310 person secure a man, or wisdom prevent 'em, or greatness exempt, or riches redeem them. But present experience hath taught us that in this case all these stand in no stead. For we see the properest men take part of them, the best wits cannot avoid them (for then should poets be no 315 cuckolds). Nor can money redeem them, for then would rich men fine for their horns, as they do for offices. But this is held for a maxim, that there are more rich cuckolds than poor. Lastly, for continuance of the horn, it is undeterminable till death. Neither do they determine with the wife's 320 death (howsoever ignorant writers hold opinion they do). For as when a knight dies, his lady still retains the title of lady; when a company is cast, yet the captain still retains the title of captain; so though the wife die, by whom this title

---

301. *the lion . . . proclamation*] a common joke in the Renaissance, apparently not one of Aesop's fables, though St. Thomas More identifies it as such. For the entire fable, see More's *History of Richard III*, ed. R. S. Sylvester (The Yale Edition of More's *Complete Works*), III, 93, 269.

309. *irrevitable*] The *OED* cites this example for its only use in English of the word *irrenitable* ("not to be struggled against"), deriving it from *ir* plus the Latin *reniti*, meaning to struggle against, resist. But it is more probably a portmanteau word incorporating *inevitable* and *irrevocable* and meaning something in between both. It does not seem to be a misprint since it occurs with the same spelling two times very close together in two separate lines.

317. *fine for*] pay money to escape.

319–320. *undeterminable*] without ending.

323. *is cast*] dismissed.

came to her husband, yet by the courtesy of the City, 325
he shall be a cuckold during life, let all ignorant asses
prate what they list.

GOSTANZO.

Notable wag! Come, sir, shake hands with him
In whose high honor you have made this speech.

MARC ANTONIO [*to* Cornelio].

And you, sir, come, join hands. Y'are one amongst them. 330

GOSTANZO.

Very well done. Now take your several wives,
And spread like wild-geese, though you now grow tame.
Live merrily together and agree,
Horns cannot be kept off with jealousy.

FINIS

EPILOGUE

Since all our labors are as you can like,
We all submit to you, nor dare presume
To think there's any real worth in them.
Sometimes feasts please the cooks, and not the guests;
Sometimes the guests, and curious cooks contemn them.   5
Our dishes we entirely dedicate
To our kind guests, but since ye differ so,
Some to like only mirth without taxations,
Some to count such works trifles, and suchlike,
We can but bring you meat, and set you stools,   10
And to our best cheer say, you all are—welcome.

---

5. *curious*] particular, fastidious.

Appendix

Chronology

Approximate years are indicated by *, occurrences in doubt by (?).

Political and Literary Events	*Life and Major Works of Chapman*
1558 Accession of Queen Elizabeth I. Robert Greene born. Thomas Kyd born.	
1560	George Chapman born in Hitchin in Hertfordshire.*
1561 Francis Bacon born.	
1564 Shakespeare born. Christopher Marlowe born.	
1572 Thomas Dekker. born.* John Donne born. Massacre of St. Bartholomew's Day.	
1573 Ben Jonson born.*	
1574 Thomas Heywood born.*	"Sent to the University" (probably Oxford, and later to Cambridge) "where he was observed to be most excellent in the Latin and Greek tongues" but "took no degree there" (Wood).*
1576 The Theatre, the first permanent public theater in London, estab-	

lished by James Burbage.
John Marston born.

1577
The Curtain theater opened.
Holinshed's *Chronicles of England,
Scotland and Ireland*.
Drake begins circumnavigation of
the earth; completed 1580.

1578
John Lyly's *Euphues: The Anatomy
of Wit*.

1579
John Fletcher born.
Sir Thomas North's translation of
Plutarch's *Lives*.

1580
Thomas Middleton born.

1583
Philip Massinger born.

1584
Francis Beaumont born.*

1586
Death of Sir Philip Sidney.
John Ford born.

1587
The Rose theater opened by
Henslowe.
Marlowe's *TAMBURLAINE*, Part
I.*
Execution of Mary, Queen of Scots.
Drake raids Cadiz.

1588
Defeat of the Spanish Armada.
Marlowe's *TAMBURLAINE*, Part
II.*

1589
Greene's *FRIAR BACON AND
FRIAR BUNGAY*.*
Marlowe's *THE JEW OF
MALTA*.*
Kyd's *THE SPANISH TRAGEDY*.*

1590

Spenser's *Faerie Queene* (Books I–III) published.

Sidney's *Arcadia* published.

Shakespeare's *HENRY VI*, Parts I–III,* *TITUS ANDRONICUS.**

1591

Shakespeare's *RICHARD III.**

In Low Countries as member of English Expeditionary Force (?).

1592

Marlowe's *DOCTOR FAUSTUS** and *EDWARD II.**

Shakespeare's *TAMING OF THE SHREW** and *THE COMEDY OF ERRORS.**

Death of Greene.

1593

Shakespeare's *LOVE'S LABOR'S LOST;** *Venus and Adonis* published.

Death of Marlowe.

Theaters closed on account of plague.

Associating with Raleigh, Roydon, Marlowe, and Harriot in the "School of Night."*

1594

Shakespeare's *TWO GENTLE-MEN OF VERONA;** *The Rape of Lucrece* published.

Shakespeare's company becomes Lord Chamberlain's Men.

Death of Kyd.

The Shadow of the Night (*Hymnus in Noctem* and *Hymnus in Cynthiam*).

1595

The Swan theater built.

Sidney's *Defense of Poesy* published.

Shakespeare's *ROMEO AND JULIET,** *A MIDSUMMER NIGHT'S DREAM,** *RICHARD II.**

Raleigh's first expedition to Guiana.

Ovid's Banquet of Sense, A Coronet for His Mistress Philosophy, and His Amorous Zodiac.

1596

Spenser's *Faerie Queene* (Books IV–VI) published.

Shakespeare's *MERCHANT OF VENICE,** *KING JOHN.**

James Shirley born.

Chapman writing for the Admiral's company.*

THE BLIND BEGGAR OF ALEXANDRIA (printed 1598).

De Guiana.

1597

Bacon's *Essays* (first edition).
Shakespeare's *HENRY IV*, Part I.*

AN HUMOROUS DAY'S MIRTH (printed 1599), a prototype of the comedy of humors.

1598

Demolition of The Theatre.*
Shakespeare's *MUCH ADO ABOUT NOTHING*,* *HENRY IV*, Part II.*
Jonson's *EVERY MAN IN HIS HUMOR* (first version).

Mentioned by Meres in *Palladis Tamia* as one of the best writers of comedy and tragedy.
Completes *Hero and Leander; Seven Books of the Iliads* (tr.); *Achilles Shield* (tr.).

1599

The Paul's Boys reopen their theater.
The Globe theater opened.
Shakespeare's *AS YOU LIKE IT*,*
*HENRY V, JULIUS CAESAR.**
Dekker's *THE SHOEMAKERS' HOLIDAY.**
Marston's *ANTONIO AND MELLIDA*,* Parts I and II.
Death of Spenser.

*ALL FOOLS** (printed 1605).

1600

Shakespeare's *TWELFTH NIGHT.**
The Fortune theater built by Alleyn.
The Children of the Chapel begin to play at the Blackfriars.

Begins writing for the recently revived children companies, Paul's Boys and the Children of the Chapel.

1601

Shakespeare's *HAMLET*,* *MERRY WIVES OF WINDSOR.**
Insurrection and execution of the Earl of Essex.
Jonson's *POETASTER.*

1602

Shakespeare's *TROILUS AND CRESSIDA.**

*THE CONSPIRACY AND TRAGEDY OF CHARLES, DUKE OF BYRON** (printed 1608); *THE GENTLEMAN USHER** (printed 1606); *SIR GILES GOOSECAP* (?)* (printed 1606).

1603

Death of Queen Elizabeth I; accession of James VI of Scotland as James I.

Florio's translation of Montaigne's *Essays* published.

Shakespeare's *ALL'S WELL THAT ENDS WELL.**

Heywood's *A WOMAN KILLED WITH KINDNESS.*

Marston's *THE MALCONTENT.**

Shakespeare's company becomes the King's Men.

1604

Shakespeare's *MEASURE FOR MEASURE,** *OTHELLO.**

Marston's *THE FAWN.**

1605

Shakespeare's *KING LEAR.**

Marston's *THE DUTCH COURTESAN.**

Bacon's *Advancement of Learning* published.

The Gunpowder Plot.

1606

Shakespeare's *MACBETH.**

Jonson's *VOLPONE.**

Tourneur's *REVENGER'S TRAGEDY.**

The Red Bull theater built.

Death of John Lyly.

1607

Shakespeare's *ANTONY AND CLEOPATRA.**

Beaumont's *KNIGHT OF THE BURNING PESTLE.**

Settlement of Jamestown, Virginia.

1608

Shakespeare's *CORIOLANUS,** *TIMON OF ATHENS,** *PERICLES.**

Becomes protégé of Prince Henry, who appoints him his "sewer in ordinary" in 1604.

*MONSIEUR D'OLIVE** (printed 1606); *BUSSY D'AMBOIS** (printed 1607).

*THE WIDOW'S TEARS** (printed 1612); *THE TRAGEDY OF CAESAR AND POMPEY** (printed 1631).

EASTWARD HO, in collaboration with Jonson and Marston (printed 1605); Chapman and Jonson imprisoned because of alleged derogatory allusions to King James.

A spring performance of the *BYRON* plays with an indecorous presentation on the stage of the

Dekker's *Gull's Hornbook* published.
Richard Burbage leases Blackfriars Theatre for King's company.
John Milton born.

1609
Shakespeare's *CYMBELINE;** Sonnets published.
Jonson's *EPICOENE.*

1610
Jonson's *ALCHEMIST.*
Richard Crashaw born.

1611
Authorized (King James) Version of the Bible published.
Shakespeare's *THE WINTER'S TALE,** *THE TEMPEST.**
Beaumont and Fletcher's *A KING AND NO KING.*
Middleton's *A CHASTE MAID IN CHEAPSIDE.**
Tourneur's *ATHEIST'S TRAGEDY.**

1612
Webster's *THE WHITE DEVIL.**

1613
The Globe theater burned.
Shakespeare's *HENRY VIII* (with Fletcher).
Webster's *THE DUCHESS OF MALFI.**
Sir Thomas Overbury murdered.

1614
The Globe theater rebuilt.
The Hope theater built.
Jonson's *BARTHOLOMEW FAIR.*

living French Queen results in vehement protests of the French Ambassador and to wholesale excisions in the printed text.

Euthymiae Raptus, or the Tears of Peace; Twelve Books of the Iliads (tr.); *MAY DAY** (printed 1611).

BUSSY D'AMBOIS revised* (printed 1641); *REVENGE OF BUSSY D'AMBOIS** (printed 1613).

The complete *Iliads* (tr.).

Petrarch's Seven Penitential Psalms [tr.] . . . *and a Hymn to Christ upon the Cross; An Epicede, or Funeral Song* (on the death on November 6 of Prince Henry).

THE MASQUE OF THE MIDDLE TEMPLE AND LINCOLN'S INN (set designed by Inigo Jones), performed on February 15 as part of the entertainment celebrating the marriage of Princess Elizabeth to Palsgrave, the Elector Palatine (printed 1613).

Eugenia; Andromeda Liberata, or The Nuptials of Perseus and Andromeda; Justification of . . . Andromeda Liberata.

1615

The complete *Odysseys* (tr.).

1616

Publication of Folio edition of Jonson's *Works*.
Death of Shakespeare.
Death of Beaumont.

The Whole Works of Homer (tr.); *Divine Poem of Musaeus* (tr.).

1618

Outbreak of Thirty Years War.
Execution of Raleigh.

Georgics of Hesiod (tr.).

1620

Settlement of Plymouth, Massachusetts.

1621–24

THE TRAGEDY OF CHABOT, ADMIRAL OF FRANCE (printed 1639).

1621

Middleton's *WOMEN BEWARE WOMEN.*
Robert Burton's *Anatomy of Melancholy* published.
Andrew Marvell born.

1622

Middleton and Rowley's *THE CHANGELING.*
Henry Vaughan born.

Pro Vere, Autumni Lachrymae.

1623

Publication of Folio edition of Shakespeare's *COMEDIES, HISTORIES, AND TRAGEDIES.*

An Invective ... against Mr. Ben Jonson.

1624.

Crown of All Homer's Works (tr.).*

1625

Death of King James I; accession of Charles I.
Death of Fletcher.

1626

Death of Tourneur.
Death of Bacon.

1627

Death of Middleton.

1628
Ford's *THE LOVER'S MELAN-CHOLY.*
Petition of Right.
Buckingham assassinated.
1629

Fifth Satire of Juvenal (tr.).

1631
Shirley's *THE TRAITOR.*
Death of Donne.
John Dryden born.
1632
Massinger's *THE CITY MADAM.**
1633
Donne's *Poems* published.
Death of George Herbert.
1634
Death of Marston, Webster.*
Publication of *THE TWO NOBLE KINSMEN,* with title-page attribution to Shakespeare and Fletcher.
Milton's *Camus.*

Chapman dies on May 12; buried in the parish of St. Giles-in-the-Fields, where Inigo Jones erects a monument to his memory.

1635
Sir Thomas Browne's *Religio Medici.*
1637
Death of Jonson.
1639
First Bishops' War.
Death of Carew.*
1640
Short Parliament.
Long Parliament inpeaches Laud.
Death of Massinger, Burton.
1641
Irish rebel.
Revision of *BUSSY D'AMBOIS* published.
Death of Heywood.
1642
Charles I leaves London; Civil War breaks out.
Shirley's *COURT SECRET.*
All theaters closed by Act of Parliament.

1643
Parliament swears to the Solemn League and Covenant.

1645
Ordinance for New Model Army enacted.

1646
End of First Civil War.

1647
Army occupies London.
Charles I forms alliance with Scots.
Publication of Folio edition of Beaumont and Fletcher's *COMEDIES AND TRAGEDIES*.

1648
Second Civil War.

1649
Execution of Charles I.

1650
Jeremy Collier born.

1651
Hobbes' *Leviathan* published.

1652
First Dutch War began (ended 1654).
Thomas Otway born.

1653
Nathaniel Lee born.*

1656
D'Avenant's *THE SIEGE OF RHODES* performed at Rutland House.

1657
John Dennis born.

1658
Death of Oliver Cromwell.
D'Avenant's *THE CRUELTY OF THE SPANIARDS IN PERU* performed at the Cockpit.

1660
Restoration of Charles II.

Theatrical patents granted to Thomas Killigrew and Sir William D'Avenant, authorizing them to form, respectively, the King's and the Duke of York's Companies.

1661
Cowley's THE CUTTER OF COLEMAN STREET.
D'Avenant's THE SIEGE OF RHODES (expanded to two parts).

1662
Charter granted to the Royal Society.

1663
Dryden's THE WILD GALLANT.
Tuke's THE ADVENTURES OF FIVE HOURS.

1664
Sir John Vanbrugh born.
Dryden's THE RIVAL LADIES.
Dryden and Howard's THE INDIAN QUEEN.
Etherege's THE COMICAL REVENGE.

1665
Second Dutch War began (ended 1667).
Great Plague.
Dryden's THE INDIAN EMPEROR.
Orrery's MUSTAPHA.

1666
Fire of London.
Death of James Shirley.